Link Em Up
on
Outlook

by Stephen J. Link

Holy Macro! Books
13386 Judy Ave. NW
Uniontown, Ohio, USA, 44685

Link Em Up on Outlook

Publisher: Bill Jelen
Book Designer: Linda DeLonais
Technical Editor: Anne Troy
Indexer: Linda DeLonais
Cover Designer: Roy Rubin

International Standard Book Number: 1-932802-01-0
Library of Congress Control Number: 2004101507
Printed in Hong Kong
First Printing: August 2004
9 8 7 6 5 4 3 2 1

About the Author

Steve Link is the owner of Link Em Up, a computer consulting company located in North Carolina in the small town of Lucama, located about fifty miles from the capital city of Raleigh.

Mr. Link has been utilizing and supporting computers for over fifteen years and has collected a few "dinosaurs" throughout that time. In his "computer museum" is an original IBM PC-XT with original monochrome monitor, plus a whopping 640k of memory and a ten-megabyte hard drive, along with a daisy wheel printer—basically a typewriter connected to a computer.

The most important thoughts gained and used throughout the years of providing user support are "Save often" and "Don't be afraid, it doesn't bite."

Steve is an active contributor of the Experts Exchange web site and ranks among the top five in their Outlook section, along with impressive rankings in other sections. He holds Microsoft's A+ certification and the Microsoft Office Specialist certification for Outlook™ 2002.

Link Em Up (www.linkemup.us) specializes in PC hardware troubleshooting and custom database programming using Visual Foxpro™. One program written by Link Em Up is called Booking Agent. Although a database program by nature—matching referees to sports games—it thoroughly utilizes the open nature of the Microsoft Office suite and uses Outlook and Outlook Express for e-mailing assignments along with Microsoft Excel spreadsheets to send data to end users.

Steve enjoys spending time with family. With two children in school, something is always happening, whether it is a soccer game, baseball game, cub scouts, etc. Without family support this book could not have been written.

Acknowledgements

I would like to thank the following for their support throughout the writing of this book. Whether through moral support or providing macro code to be included in the automation section, those mentioned here provided much needed support.

God ("With Him all things are possible") and my church

Anne Troy—Thanks for the opportunity, encouragement, and support

Tonia Link—my wife. Thanks for being there for me through everything in life.

Stephane Friggeri—for providing the automation code for Custom E-mail from Excel and Exploding E-mail)

Bill Jelen of www.MrExcel.com

SnagIt from www.TechSmith.com

Craig Kirby for writing a great Foreword

All of the users at www.ExpertsExchange.com for the experience and capabilities gained through their help site (I hope I was able to give as much or more than I gained).

The many teachers I have had in my life. We consider our teachers to be those we learned from while in school. We learn new things every day. I learn from my children on a regular basis.

Table of Contents

Foreword

Communication is the outgrowth of humankind's need and desire to interact. From the sharing of ideas and data to expressions of personal and emotional thought, we have developed many means to communicate with others.

Ancient man made crude drawings on cave walls and developed primitive languages. Succeeding generations refined verbal and written communication, but the basic structure of communication has remained constant for most of known history. The only thing that changes over time is the *method* used to transmit information.

The dawning of the 21st Century finds mankind communicating more prolifically than any time in history, through the use of *E-mail*. E-mail applications, such as Outlook, are all about communication.

The US government began the development of a network-based system of communication in the early seventies, transmitting the first e-mail message over ARPANET in 1971. It was the personal computer (PC) that enabled this new technology to be used by the masses, and new devices such as laptops and hand-held PCs have made "e-mail" the simplest and most efficient way in history to communicate.

Outlook is the most widely used e-mail application today. Its ease of use and adaptability enables millions of people to share ideas, thoughts and data with a few keystrokes, and it takes place *instantly*. So fire up that PC, and communicate!

Craig Kirby
July 2004

This page intentionally left blank.

1. Discussion on Outlook

Outlook is the most versatile e-mail program available from Microsoft. It is quite capable of scheduling your day, keeping up with your Rolodex®, and handling both basic and advanced e-mail jobs and has been since the '97 version.

Outlook goes well beyond this basic functionality in also allowing you to send meeting requests that can be accepted, declined, or have alternate times proposed. Other items that you can schedule include meeting rooms and other resources.

Another great feature is the ability to create recurring items. Using this, you could schedule an employee meeting on a specific day of every month. You could even schedule one for the fourth Thursday of every month!

Notes are another handy feature in Outlook. Some people have the monitor littered with "sticky notes". Instead of this cluttered desk space, they could be using Notes within Outlook.

The journal is a useful part of Outlook, too. You can use it to track phone calls, e-mails, documents, and many other events related to a contact. The timer is quite handy for billing support call time.

While the calendar is helpful in planning your day, tasks help you to track your "honey-do" lists and any other assignments you may have. You can add anything you want and give it a specific due date with a reminder date and time.

Popular Features

In this section we'll briefly discuss some of the features offered by Outlook. These features are the driving reasons behind the popularity of Personal Information Managers (PIMs).

A basic e-mail job is something that everyone uses. You compose an e-mail, address it, and send it.

An advanced e-mail job might be something that is automatically generated from a program or it could be a carefully formatted "composition." We'll cover both of these scenarios in later chapters (see Basic E-mail Options on page 5-5 and Advanced E-mail Options on page 5-6).

Sending/Receiving e-mail is only a part of the e-mail side of Outlook. Management of your e-mail is a large portion of the duties that Outlook handles. One handy management tool is the implementation of rules and alerts.

Great Features

The Favorites Folder in Outlook 2003 greatly helps you to manage large volumes of e-mail. You can create special folders and have rules in place to automatically separate the incoming e-mail into these folders based on title, recipient, and so forth. The Favorite Folders display in their own section together.

Something else that is quite helpful in the management of your e-mail is the ability to customize the commands and features you see in the toolbars.

The Mailbox Cleanup Wizard is another useful function. It helps you to utilize your mailbox space as efficiently as possible. Later, we'll go through cleaning up, archiving, and deleting of items (see Using the Mailbox Cleanup Wizard on page 9-28).

Version-specific Features

Outlook 2000 had the following features:

➢ Most Recently Used (MRU) List—under the File menu selection; this list provides quick access to the folders open with the File–Open menu item

➢ Improved appearance and functionality of the printed calendar

➢ Resting the mouse pointer over an appointment in the daily or workweek view displays the entire text of that appointment (when you can't see the whole thing in the regular display area)

➢ Option of using Microsoft Word™ as the e-mail editor; provides many formatting options not previously available

➢ Save the calendar as a web page to be viewed by others

➢ Create groups of contacts called Personal Distribution Lists; allows you to send a message to many people at once by selecting a group instead of individuals

➢ Mail merge to Word—provides capability to merge an e-mail just like you would merge a form letter

Outlook 2002 (also called XP or version 11) added some more features:

- Much better Preview Pane
- AutoSuggest addresses makes addressing e-mail much easier
- Improved integration of WordMail (using MSWord as the editor)

Outlook 2003 (version 12) added even more helpful features:

- Major user interface changes and improvements
- Easier to use Rules Wizard
- Safe and Block lists for spam control
- Increased Speed for e-mail sending and receiving
- Meeting Workplace for scheduling meetings
- View contact's picture in their record

Groans And Moans

- Vulnerability to viruses
  Outlook's popularity has caused it to be the target of most virus writers. Many attempts have been made to clamp down on the spread of viruses through e-mail. The implementation of security features has gotten to the point that it stands in the way of real productivity. User awareness and updated virus-scanning software are the best means to prevent the virus infections that seem to be so common and widespread.
- Autoformatting needs to be improved
- Outlook coming to the forefront of your computer and interrupting whatever you are doing when new mail is received
- Junk Mail handling capabilities are greatly lacking
- Spell check should look at the subject line in addition to the e-mail itself.

Some of these issues have been addressed in the 2003 version of Outlook.

Praises for Outlook 2003

Some of these features were also available in previous versions.

- Ease of use; beginners can jump right in and create contacts and e-mails

> Different types of help available—Via the web and through the Office Assistants (the paperclip, Einstein, or whomever else you may choose)

> Ability to import from and export to other e-mail programs (Microsoft and Non-Microsoft)

> Easy to program from Visual Basic™, Visual Foxpro™, Microsoft™ Word, and other Microsoft products

> Autoformatting can be customized to fit the user's writing style

> Junk mail handling capabilities are improved due to the ability to set safe senders and recipients

2. Exchange Server 2003

When an Exchange Server is used, mail comes into a common server (computer) and is distributed to client users using Exchange Server software. Exchange Servers are generally handled by Mail Administrators. However, you should be aware of some Exchange Server settings that commonly affect users.

> Note: Client-side generally refers to the user's PC when the user is at work and an Exchange Server is in use. In this book, it may also refer to your PC as the user of Outlook. Server-side means the Exchange Server, not Outlook running on a PC.

Here are just a few of the settings that can be made or changed by your Mail Server administrator.

> * *Maximum amount of mailbox storage space.* Many companies restrict the amount to a default value—for instance, 20 Meg. You may receive huge attachment files regularly and require more space. Proper disk usage management allows specific users to have more space based on specific requirements.

> * *Out of Office Assistant (OOA).* Some companies do not allow the use of this feature. The OOA is only available in Outlook when an Exchange Server is present; it is not dependent on your PC receiving mail. If your company does not allow OOA usage, there should be a policy that requires employees' PCs to be running to execute any rules and enable automated replies.

> * *A feature that prevents sending an OOA message if the TO or CC line is not filled in.* The main purpose of this new feature of Outlook 2003 is to keep you from replying to news lists and other automated mailing lists.

> * *The Internet Mail Wizard* greatly simplifies the configuration of Internet Mail Connectivity compared to previous versions of Exchange Server.

> * *Outlook Web Access* (discussed in later chapters, see Exchange Server Accounts on page 3-4 and Sharing Outlook Objects on page 9-14) allows for remote usage of the Exchange Server features. The user could be in Australia and access the company calendar, contacts, and e-mail just as if he or she were doing it from the office at work.

Retention Policies

Retention Policies determine the ways in which an Exchange Server can be set to retain deleted items for a specific number of days. When items are removed from the Deleted Items folder, they are still available for recall during that specified period—generally one to three weeks. Your Exchange Server administrator sets the appropriate policies.

A question asked repeatedly in support groups is how to recover items that have been emptied from the Deleted Items folder. The answer is that it cannot be done without the Exchange Server present and Retention Policies in use. Keep this in mind whenever emptying the Deleted Items folder.

Distribution Lists

A *Distribution List* is a group of recipients that have something in common. For instance, in a company of five hundred people, there may be twenty-five in the marketing department. If you wanted to send correspondence to everyone in that department, you could group all of their e-mail addresses together in a Distribution List named Marketing.

Suppose you want to send to ALMOST everyone in that list. Outlook 2003 provides a method of doing this; however, it requires a registry edit.

WARNING! Careless editing of the registry can render your operating system useless. Registry editing should be performed with extreme caution.

The *Expand List* feature allows you to display the recipients in a Distribution List directly in the recipient boxes (the To, the CC, and the BCC boxes). After expanding the Distribution List, the recipient box of your e-mail message displays the resolved names of all members.

When you expand a Distribution List, Outlook displays the following message is:

```
If you expand the list, Outlook will replace the list with
its members. You will not be able to collapse it again.
```

The Expand List dialog box is controlled by the following registry key:

```
HKEY_CURRENT_USER\Software\Microsoft\Office\11.0\
Outlook\Options\General
```

Setting the PONT_STRING value to 13 hides the Expand List dialog box. Changing the PONT_STRING value to something other than 13 causes the Expand List dialog box to appear. The PONT_STRING value resides in the registry key noted above it.

The default REG_SZ string value for the PONT_STRING value is "32,". Note that the default value includes the comma.

Keep the following in mind when expanding a Distribution List:

➢ Most mail servers limit the maximum number of recipients that an e-mail message can contain. Exceeding this limit causes a non-delivery receipt and failure in sending the message.

➢ Once you expand a Distribution List, you cannot collapse it again.

➢ There are no client-side configuration options or limits available for the Expand List feature. If an Exchange Server is not configured for Expand List in Outlook, this feature is not available.

➢ Client-side Distribution List expansion cannot be turned off, but it can be regulated by the mail server's Max Recipients configuration. Exchange 2000 and Exchange 2003 Servers have the default Max Recipients value set at 5000. Most consumer ISPs have a limit of 10 recipients set. Your mail administrator can configure this option in the Exchange System Manager (ESM) properties of Message Delivery (global settings).

➢ Whenever Outlook 2003 expands a large Distribution List, its performance may decline as it extracts the addresses and populates the individual recipients. The speed and memory of the computer greatly determines how fast this process is performed.

Tip: Pay special attention to the warnings about editing the registry and the fact that expanded lists will no longer display the list name only.

This page intentionally left blank.

3. Installing Outlook

Types of Installations

Now we'll cover the different types of Outlook installation. The most popular personal configuration for Outlook uses the POP3 (Post Office Protocol) and/or HTTP (Hyper-Text Transfer Protocol) accounts. IMAP (Internet Mail Access Protocol) could be used for business or personal application, though the use of that type of account is slowly fading out. Most mid-size and large businesses use Microsoft Exchange Server. Exchange Server allows for efficient management and sharing of all aspects of the Outlook program.

Setting up POP3 Accounts

If you install Outlook for home use, you would use a POP3-type server to connect to your Internet Service Provider's (ISP) mail server. Click on Tools–E-mail Accounts–Add a new account; a dialog appears from which you can choose the server type options mentioned above.

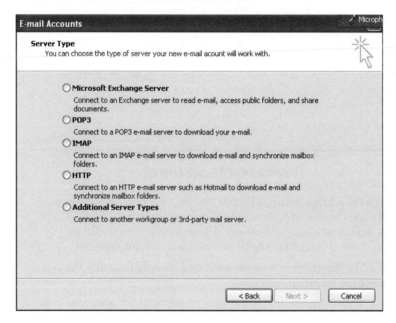

Figure 3-1 Selecting Server Type

A mail server is simply a computer that stores mail. As already stated, POP3 is the method your computer uses to connect to your ISP's mail server. Your ISP should provide a user name, password, and incoming and outgoing server names.

The SMTP (Simple Mail Transfer Protocol) server name is the server that is used to SEND your e-mail, while the POP3 server is used to RECEIVE your mail. Many ISPs use the same server address for both sending and receiving.

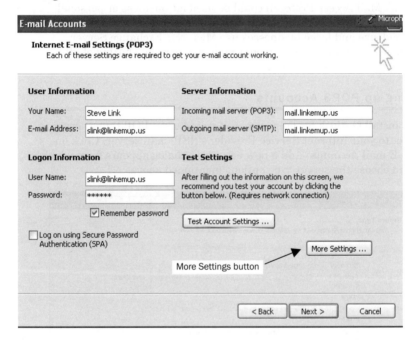

Figure 3-2 POP3 E-mail Settings

You also have a More Settings button (see above). This allows you to set up additional options on your account, such as organization, reply address, default account, and others. These settings are useful in providing more information to the receiver, but are not required.

You can add a directory or address book by following basically the same procedure used for e-mail accounts:

```
Tools-E-mail Accounts-Add a new directory or address book
```

This dialog provides for the addition of an LDAP (Lightweight Directory Access Protocol) or an additional address book. LDAP is basically an Internet address directory that may be provided by your ISP or network administrator.

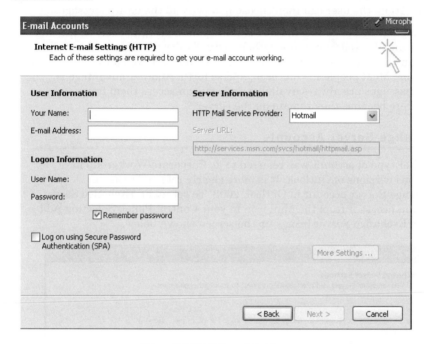

Figure 3-3 HTTP E-mail Settings

Setting up HTTP Accounts

Another type of personal e-mail account is HTTP. This is used for the web-based e-mail services such as Hotmail™, Yahoo™, and MSN™. When adding an HTTP service, select an HTTP Service Provider.

If you are using Hotmail or MSN, the Server URL is already properly configured. You need to provide your name, e-mail address, user name, and password. If you choose Other, you must also provide the correct Server URL address. An example is:

```
http://services.msn.com/svcs/hotmail/httpmail.asp
```

IMAP Accounts

All e-mail in an IMAP account is stored on the server and only the headers (From, To, Subject) are downloaded. After viewing the header information, the user can then choose to download the entire message.

One big advantage to this method is that spam mail can be left on the server and deleted from there without actually downloading it. After all, you can identify most spam by the subject—You have won a free vacation, Meet people in your area, and so forth. Another advantage is that messages are always available and you can access them from anywhere because they remain on the server.

Exchange Server Accounts

Another type of account was referred to as Corporate/Workgroup in previous versions of Outlook. It is more clearly referred to as an Exchange Server account in Outlook 2003. To set up an Exchange Server account, access it from the Mail icon in your Control Panel. Selecting Add a new Exchange Server brings up the screen shown below.

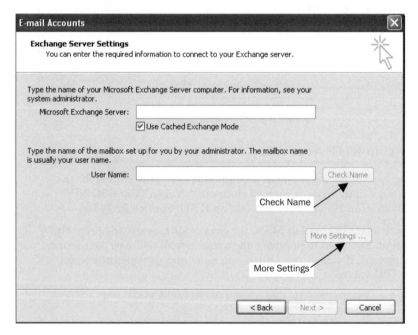

Figure 3-4 Exchange Server Settings

In the Exchange Server text box, insert the name of the Exchange Server on your network. User Name goes in the second box. Clicking on Check Name causes Outlook to connect to the server and verify that the name exists as an account on the Exchange server. The More Settings button brings up a standard Exchange Server properties box.

This section explained how to set up a public folder in Exchange Server. Keep in mind that some things vary from version to version. The version we used here was Exchange 2003.

Setting up Different Address Books on the Same Account

Perhaps you want to share your computer and e-mail account with another family member, but you both want different address books. The following figure is the dialog for adding another PST address book to your account.

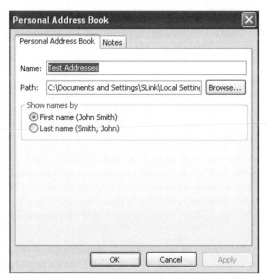

Figure 3-5 Personal Address Book Settings

These settings are relatively self-explanatory. An address book can be named anything you choose, but be sure to give each one a unique name so it can be easily distinguished from the others. Address books can also reside in different directories. The default location shown in the Path box is recommended to make sure that all address books are located in the same place.

Notice the two options for displaying contact names. The default selection sorts by first name, but some users may prefer to have the address book sorted by last name instead.

The Notes tab has an area where you can type anything you wish to describe this address book and distinguish it from any others.

Installing an Upgrade

The most likely installation you'll have is an upgrade. Since most users purchase the entire Office suite, we will cover the steps for upgrading the current version of Office to the new Office 2003.

After inserting the CD, the installation files are automatically copied to the hard drive and the install wizard begins.

1. Enter the 25-character product key. It is generally located on the inside or back of the CD case. Click Next.

2. Enter your name, initials, and organization (if for a business). It is important to enter the initials in this step because they are used in some of the Office programs for document properties. Click Next.

3. Read the license agreement and signify that you accept the terms and conditions by checking the appropriate box. By paying close attention to the license and the specifications on the box, you may discover that the software can be installed on multiple computers under certain conditions. Click Next.

4. Now you must make some choices. The default (and most common) setting is a *Typical Install*. It installs the most common components of Office. Office tools (such as spell checker, grammar and thesaurus proofing tools) are included with the typical install. Keep in mind that any additional necessary components will be requested, as they are required.

    The *Minimal Install* is not recommended. It generally works well if hard drive space is severely limited, but with today's multi-gigabyte hard drives, this should not be a problem.

    The final selection is *Complete Install*. This option (as the name implies) installs every component in the Office suite. It even installs all converters and tools. If there may ever be a need to have quick access to every feature and function of Office, this type of installation is more suitable. If you choose one of the other two options and a component is needed later, the opportunity to install it will be presented at that time.

You should be familiar with the software packages available (depending on the specific edition): Word, Excel™, PowerPoint™, Outlook, Access™, Publisher™, FrontPage™, InfoPath™, OneNote™, Project™, and Visio™. Some of the tools and converters available are: Analysis Toolpak™, Lookup Wizard™, Solver™, Lotus Organizer™ converter, various stationery, clip organizer, document update utilities, and many more.

Activating Outlook

After completing the installation, it is necessary to activate your software. This can be accomplished by clicking first on the Help menu and then on Activate Product. It is important that the product be activated with Microsoft because there is a limit to the number of times the application can be used before requiring activation.

Compatible Versions

Note that two versions of Outlook (one being Outlook 2003) cannot successfully run on one PC, even though other applications can successfully run with multiple versions installed.

Outlook 2003 is also incompatible with older versions of Word. Use careful consideration before purchasing a stand-alone version of Outlook 2003. When choosing Word as your e-mail editor in Outlook 2003, remember that you can only successfully use the 2003 version of Word.

This page intentionally left blank.

4. Outlook Menu Overview

Office menu systems are, by default, designed to move the most often used menu items to the top of the dropdown menu list. The usual way to display all menu items is to leave the mouse cursor over one of the menu items for a few seconds or click on the double arrows at the bottom of the menu. Either action expands the menu to show all menu items. To always view all of the items under the menus, go to Tools-Customize and choose Options. Make sure "Always show full menus" is checked.

File Menu

There are many file management options under the File menu. We'll only discuss those that are not self-explanatory.

Figure 4-1 File Menu

> *New*   Expands out to create a new item, which could be an e-mail, contact, or even an Internet fax

> *Open*   Expands out to include items such as Selected Items, Other User's Folder, and Outlook Data File

> *Save As*   Allows saving of the selected item in a specified format (such as Text Only, Outlook Template, Outlook Message Format)

> *Folder*   Expands out to add a folder, rename a folder, or view the properties of a folder

> *Data File   Brings up the Outlook Data Files screen you see below
> Management*   On this screen, you can create, add, and modify mailbox files. If you have an Outlook PST file from a friend to add into your Outlook, you can add it here. Separate mail folders are displayed in the All Mail Folders display area.

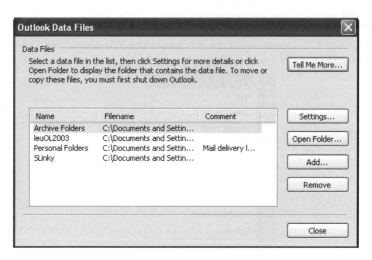

Figure 4-2 Data File Management Screen

> *Import and   Allows import from or export to other formats
> Export*

> *Archive*   Allows manual archiving of data in selected folders

The archive option brings up the Archive screen shown on the following page. This screen gives you the ability to specify the archive settings. Choose the folder, date, and location, and click OK. To access the ability to permanently delete archived items, you must go to the Properties of the folder by right-clicking it.

Figure 4-3 Archive Screen

Edit Menu

You will find the standard Windows editing functionality, such as copy, paste, delete, undo, and move, under the Edit menu (see the Figure on the following page).

In addition, you'll find these Outlook-specific functions.

> *Mark As Read* and   Changes the status of the message(s) selected
> *Mark As Unread*

> *Categories*   Described in detail in the Contacts section
>   See Categories on page 8-30.

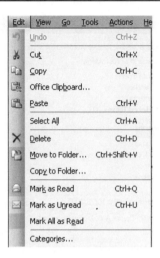

Figure 4-4 Edit Menu

View Menu

The View menu gives you many options for arranging your data. The View menu is shown on the following page.

> *Arrange By*   Allows modification of the sort, filter, and group settings

> *Navigation Pane*   Toggle on or off by clicking on menu item

> *Reading Pane*   Expands out to set the Pane to right, bottom, or off

> *AutoPreview*   Toggle on or off by clicking on menu item

> *Expand/Collapse Groups*   Expand or collapses groups in the current folder

> *Reminders Window*   Displays any upcoming appointments

> *Toolbars*   Expands out to choose which toolbars are displayed

> *Status Bar*   Toggle on or off by clicking on menu item

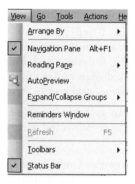

Figure 4-5 View Menu

Go Menu

Go provides another method for opening folders. If the Navigation Pane is displayed, you can select a folder, such as Mail, Calendar, or Contacts, simply by clicking on it.

Figure 4-6 Go Menu

Tools Menu

Tools is the most powerful menu in Outlook. See the Figure on the following page.

> *Send/receive*   Choose sending and receiving options on specific mailboxes

The rest of the features available in the Tools menu are explained in more detail throughout this book. Briefly, however, the Tools menu allows you to change the appearance and handling of Outlook's folders (such as E-mail and Junk E-mail, Calendar and Journal, Tasks, Contacts, and Notes). It lets you design and configure Forms and Macros, customize your Outlook application, and access your Address Book.

Conduit Manager may be on your system if you have a Personal Digital Assistant such as an IPAQ or Palm connected with and synchronized to Outlook.

The Tools menu helps you to organize Outlook using folders, colors, and views, automatically add holidays to your calendar, schedule resources, and even set up spell check options. Click around on the various screens under Tools. You'll be glad you familiarized yourself with its options.

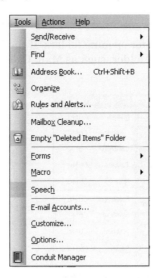

Figure 4-7 Tools Menu

Actions Menu

The Actions menu provides many options that are also available from the toolbars or from right-click menus (also called Context menus).

The Actions menu changes, based on the type of folder you have chosen. In this example, I selected the Mail folder.

Figure 4-8 Actions Menu with Mail folder Selected

> *New Mail Message*   Creates a new, blank e-mail

> *New Mail Message*   Shows the many options you have for creating
> *Using*   a new message

For example, a new message created with the
Microsoft Excel Worksheet selection is actually
a blank Excel spreadsheet with e-mail
recipient information above it. You get to
create the Excel spreadsheet, just as you would
within the program.

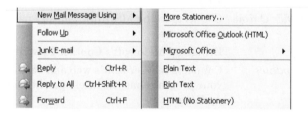

Figure 4-9 New Mail Message Using Menu

> *Follow Up*   Sets or modifies the follow-up flag on the
selected item

> *Junk E-mail*   Allows the addition of the selected e-mail
address (or domain) to the junk e-mail list

> *Reply*   Replies to the selected e-mail

> *Reply to All*   Replies to all addresses in the selected e-mail

> *Forward*   Forward the selected e-mail to one or more
recipients

Help Menu

The final menu is Help. Outlook follows the Windows standard of attaching Help to the F1 key.

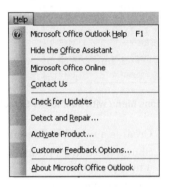

Figure 4-10 Help Menu

➢ *Office Assistant*	Office Assistant is used by default
	If you don't like the Office Assistant, you can hide it. See Using the Office Assistant on page 10-3.
➢ *Microsoft Office Online*	Connects to the MSOffice web site using your web browser
➢ *Contact Us*	Brings up Microsoft's Contact Us web page
➢ *Check For Updates*	Connects to Microsoft's web and verifies that your program has the latest patches and updates
➢ *Detect and Repair*	Runs a program that repairs and fixes problems with your Outlook installation. It may require the insertion of your installation disks

5. Settings

This section takes you through some of the myriad settings you can use to control Outlook's appearance and operation.

General Settings

To configure general settings, click on Tools–Customize. Now click the Options tab. You can perform the following actions:

➢ Select between always show full menus and show full menus after a short delay

➢ Reset menu and toolbar usage data
Clears out the items automatically listed at the top of the menus. These items are placed at the top based on their usage.

➢ Toggle large icons on or off

➢ Show font names in their actual font

➢ Show screen tips on toolbars

➢ Show shortcut keys in screen tips

➢ Change menu animations

The screen tips are really helpful. If the actual function of an icon is unknown, hovering the mouse cursor over it brings up a screen tip that displays the button's function.

Changing menu animations could be necessary if the system running Outlook is performing poorly. From any other Office 2003 application, choose Tools–Customize–Options tab, and you can change the menu animation settings.

Click on the Toolbars tab to select which toolbars are displayed. Checking the box displays a toolbar, and un-checking the box hides it. The two that should be most useful to everyone are Menu bar (which can't be hidden) and the Standard toolbar.

The Advanced and Web toolbars can also be displayed. The Advanced toolbar allows quick access to some of the more heavily used options such as AutoPreview, Rules and Alerts, and Reading Pane.

Customizing Toolbars and Menus

There may be additional custom toolbars on your computer that can be hidden or displayed. On my system, there is a toolbar called SnagIt®. It is present because of the SnagIt screen capture program I used for this book. Like SnagIt, some programs install their own toolbars into your applications.

Creating and Customizing a Toolbar

Now we are going to create a custom toolbar and add the most frequently used buttons to it. You are welcome to follow the same procedures to customize this toolbar to be more suitable for your own uses.

1. Click on the New button, name the toolbar, and click OK.

    Note the new empty toolbar. We plan on using it as the only toolbar, so it will have New and some other heavily used commands.

2. Click the Commands tab. Select the File category and the New command and drag it onto the new toolbar.

3. Now scroll down these options and choose other options that are useful. Keep in mind that every type of item is listed under New, so it is not necessary to add each individual item to the toolbar.

    After adding four items from the File category, the menu looks like this:

Figure 5-1 Custom Toolbar with File Menu Items

4. Now, on to the Edit category. The most useful commands here are delete and undo, so that is all we'll add from here. Drag them in. Now the toolbar looks like this:

Figure 5-2 Custom Toolbar with File and Edit Menu Items

5. After going through these two categories, you should have the basic idea. I'll leave you on your own to add as many as you want. The custom toolbar I created for this book is broken into two pieces for ease of reading and looks like this:

Figure 5-3 Custom Toolbar with All Menu Items

This toolbar contains the following functions, starting from the left:

1. New E-mail
2. Reply
3. Reply to all
4. Forward
5. New Contact
6. Choose Form (used for sending a new e-mail based on a template that has already been set up – more on how to create this later)
7. Delete
8. Undo
9. Choose Current View
10. Sort
11. Filter
12. Group
13. Go to inbox
14. Go to calendar
15. Send/Receive
16. Find
17. Organize
18. Rules and alerts
19. Speech (Yes, you can talk to your Outlook!)
20. Junk E-mail
21. Check For Updates (it is important to keep Outlook current)
22. Follow Up
23. Arrange By

Note the vertical dots on the left side of the menu in the top screen shot. Grabbing these with the mouse allows you to move the menu around. It can also be undocked—placed anywhere on the screen instead of staying at the top.

Notice the two dots with the down arrow at the far right of the menu (bottom menu screen shot). Clicking here allows modification of the buttons shown on the menu and displays a screen similar to the screen shot below.

Figure 5-4 Modifying Buttons

Customizing a Menu

You can customize menus in the same fashion as toolbars. Find a command you want to add to a menu and drag it to the menu. Hold it there briefly; the menu opens up so the command can now be placed in the desired position on that menu.

You can modify the order of items in a menu or toolbar by clicking on the Rearrange Command button (located below the Categories and Commands windows on the customize screen). That screen is shown below.

Figure 5-5 Rearrange Commands Screen

On the Rearrange Commands screen, you can move items on menu bars and toolbars up or down; you can also add or delete the items. The Modify Selection button allows many modifications to the currently selected item. These are listed below:

> Reset

> Delete

> Name

> Default Style

> Text Only, Image and Text

> Begin a Group

- Copy, paste, reset, edit, and change button image
- Assign Hyperlink

The first three options in the list (Reset, Delete, and Name) are the only options available for menu items. The whole list applies to toolbar items. You can change the button image, add hyperlinks to web pages, and even create new command groups. The only limit to the customization of menus and toolbars is your imagination.

Recommended Settings

This section takes you through various configuration options and explains which ones you should choose in order to get the most out of Outlook with the least trouble. Select Tools–Options–E-mail Options.

Basic E-mail Options

- *Close original message on Reply or Forward* (unchecked)

  This option leaves the message on the screen when replying or forwarding instead of automatically closing it.

- *Save copies of messages in Sent Items folder* (checked)

  You will probably find yourself looking through this folder many times to verify what you sent in a message to a client.

- *Automatically save unsent messages* (unchecked)

  If your practice is to create an e-mail just to see how a font would appear or to show a friend what neat stuff you gained from your favorite new book, this should be unchecked.

  With it checked, every message exited without being sent is automatically saved in the Drafts folder. Clearing this checkbox causes a prompt to display every time you close an unsent message.

- *Remove extra line breaks in plain text messages* (checked)

  Choose this option to make sure that the e-mails are properly formatted when they are displayed in the Reading Pane and when they are opened.

- *Read all standard mail in plain text* (unchecked)

  With this option checked, incoming e-mail will not be seen exactly as it was composed.

- *When Replying (and Forwarding) a message*

  Include original message text. This keeps the message text with the reply or forward.

	One useful example is for the recipient to be able to review a question you are answering.
➢ *Mark my comments with* (unchecked)	Comments get quite bothersome when you receive a message that has been forwarded five times. The indents and > characters make it basically unreadable. Avoid the "Prefix each line with" option LIKE THE PLAGUE!!!!

Advanced E-mail Options

➢ *Save Unsent items in Drafts*	*Saving in Drafts* is the best choice because these e-mails can be easily deleted when they are no longer useful.
➢ *Autosave unsent every xx minutes* (checked)	Autosave is always a good thing to have in case of a power outage or unavoidable computer problem. The default of three minutes is a safe interval.
➢ *Save replies with original message* (unchecked)	Use this option to save replies in folders other than the Inbox
➢ *Save forwarded messages* (checked)	For historical and review purposes, this is a good option to have checked. Set the Sent Items folder to autoarchive every couple of weeks to remove the extra e-mails accumulated there.
➢ *When new items arrive in my inbox* (check all)	*Play a sound,* if checked, alerts you that a new e-mail has arrived even though you are working on something away from the computer.
	Briefly change the mouse cursor provides a brief visual reminder that e-mail has arrived.
	Show an envelope icon in the notification area is quite handy in case you were away from your desk. The envelope acts as a reminder when you return.
	Display a desktop mail alert (default inbox only) is quite handy because a preview is displayed briefly just above your taskbar in the right corner. The desktop alert settings determine how long the preview displays and sets the transparency level.

> *Set Importance (and Sensitivity) to Normal*

Everyone has heard the story of the boy who cried wolf. Setting these to something other than Normal is quite similar.

If every message someone receives from a particular sender is high importance, that setting will eventually be ignored. When a truly important message arrives, it will not receive the urgency it deserves.

> *Messages expire after xx days* (unchecked)

This gives you control over messages after they are received.

Note that this option requires Exchange Server by both the sender and the receiver

> *Allow comma as address separator* (checked)

This option, combined with *Automatic name checking* and *Suggest names*, sure makes entering e-mail addresses easy.

> *Automatic name checking* (checked)

Compares typed portion to contact addresses and sent-e-mail addresses and automatically fills in the first match found.

> *Delete meeting request from inbox when responding* (checked)

A meeting request is no longer needed once you have accepted or denied it.

> *Suggest names while completing To, CC, and BCC fields* (checked)

Helps tremendously when entering previously used e-mail addresses.

> *Add properties to attachments to enable reply with changes* (unchecked)

Keep option unchecked (default) to protect your personal information. Checking it allows personal information (such as the name of the person editing the attached document) to be included in Office attachments sent through e-mail.

Tracking Options

> *Process requests and responses on arrival* (checked)

This option gives lets you automatically process a meeting request (saving time and keystrokes). Microsoft recommends turning this off if you are a delegate of someone else's calendar.

> *Process receipts on arrival* (checked)

This is checked by default. It also saves time.

> *After Processing move receipts to* (unchecked) — The default is unchecked. This option could save you quite a bit of time if you have request delivery and read receipts moved automatically.

> *Delete blank voting and meeting responses after processing* (checked) — Another time saver if you are in an office environment and utilize Outlook for requesting and scheduling meetings.

> *For all messages I send request read / delivery receipt* (both unchecked) — It is only good to have these checked if you are troubleshooting e-mail sending problems; otherwise, the many receipts you get back become quite irritating.

> *Use this option to decide how to respond to requests for read receipts* — *Always send, Never send*, and *Ask before sending* are the three choices here. If you are a really private person, choose never send. For the cases where you may actually want to allow sending a read receipt, the best option is ask before sending.

Junk E-mail Options

> *Set these options depending on how bothered you are by junk e-mail* (affectionately known as spam). — The default setting is Low. It should work well for most people.

If spam is a real problem, you can select safe lists only. This will reject all e-mail that is not from a domain or address you have verified as safe.

> The *Safe Senders, Safe Recipients*, and *Blocked Senders* tabs are used to set up the *safe lists*. — The Safe Senders, Safe Recipients, and Blocked Senders settings are used to crack down on the amount of spam received. You can take spam protection to the point where you only receive e-mail from someone on the Safe Senders and/or Safe Recipients list.

Calendar Options

> *Check the days of the week to view in the workweek view of the calendar* — The default is to leave the weekends out (normally Saturday and Sunday).

➤ *Show week numbers in the Date Navigator* (unchecked)	This is the default setting. Showing week numbers adds extra clutter to the view.
➤ *Allow attendees to propose new times for meetings you organize* (checked)	This is a nice option to utilize. If you propose a meeting time that is unavailable for a few attendees, they can respond with a suggested time that is better for them.
➤ *Planner Options*	Allows you to select how the planner works in scheduling meetings and group schedules.
➤ *Add Holidays* is extremely useful.	Adds the standard holidays (based on the country you choose) to your calendar.
➤ The *Time Zone settings* are of extreme importance.	If the time zone is set improperly, it will throw off e-mail sending/receiving times and will make it impossible to schedule meetings accurately. There is also an option to use Daylight Savings Time.

Mail Setup

➤ *Send/Receive immediately when connected* (checked)	This adds to the efficiency of your e-mail experience. With this option checked, your new e-mails should be sent immediately (or almost immediately if you are using a dial-up Internet connection).

E-mail Format

There are many formats that can be used for new e-mails. If you have Word 2003 installed, you can use it as the e-mail editor. This is the default setting. The standard Outlook Editor has many new features compared to previous versions, but it is not as feature-rich as Word 2003.

This section also covers the different types of e-mail formatting – HTML, Rich Text, and plain text.

Word as the E-mail Editor

You have an option to use Word2003 as the e-mail-editing program (if Word 2003 is installed). Note the two checkboxes in the following Figure.

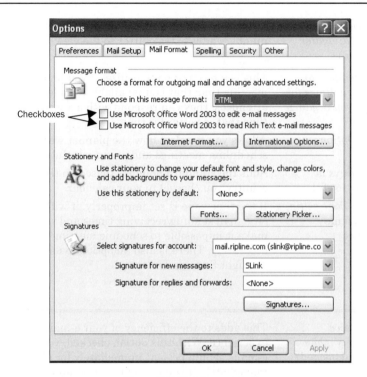

Figure 5-6 Mail Format Options

Using Word as the e-mail editor gives you all of the formatting options that are available in Microsoft Word. You can even choose Styles and Themes to create a "desktop publisher-quality" e-mail.

See the following page for a beautifully formatted newsletter e-mail we are using to introduce this book.

Announcing
L i n k   E m   U P
On Outlook

If you need help on Outlook 2000, 2002, or 2003 we have a perfect resource for you. It is for the
intermediate user.
That description should cover at least half of the Outlook user community.

It covers many features including the different types of accounts, contacts, and even Outlook
Automation.

This could be just what you need to move your career to the next level.

Call 252-252-1234 to reserve your copy now.

Hurry!! Supplies are limited

Figure 5-7 Publisher Quality E-mail

The main problem you might encounter when using this format would be
with the recipient's setup. Below you see this e-mail as it might actually
display on a recipient's computer.

```
Announcing

L i n k   E m   U p

On Outlook


If you need help on Outlook 2000, 2002, or 2003 we have a perfect resource for you.  It is for the intermediate user.

That description should cover at least half of the Outlook user community.


It covers many features including the different types of accounts, contacts, and even Outlook Automation.


This could be just what you need to move your career to the next level.

 |


Call 252-252-1234 to reserve your copy now.


Hurry!! Supplies are limited
```

Figure 5-8 Plain Text E-mail

Notice that it looks nothing like the "publisher-quality" original. The
reason for the poor appearance is that this e-mail is displayed in *Plain
Text* format. The point behind this illustration is to remind you that you
can't control the format of your recipients' computers. They may have
their program set to receive all e-mail in plain text format. In this case,
the time spent on formatting the e-mail is wasted.

Another potential problem that could arise with publisher-quality e-mail is that the recipient might not have the same fonts that you used to compose it. The e-mail might still look good, but it would not appear exactly as you originally formatted it.

Even if you're not using Word as the editor, there are still quite a few formatting options available, though nowhere near as many as you have with WordMail.

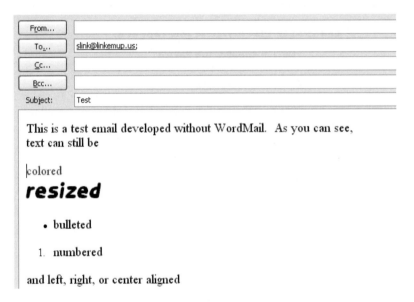

From...

To... | slink@linkemup.us;

Cc...

Bcc...

Subject: | Test

This is a test email developed without WordMail. As you can see, text can still be

colored

resized

- bulleted

1. numbered

and left, right, or center aligned

Figure 5-9 Non-WordMail E-mail

Although some of the snazzy formatting is missing, the basics are still there. You also still have to take the same precautions – you can't control the fonts and layout of the recipient's e-mail software, so your hard work may not be seen by all of the people who receive it.

Adding a Signature

In most e-mail programs, you have something known as a signature. A signature consists of text and/or graphics placed at the end of every e-mail you send. You'll find an example signature on the following page.

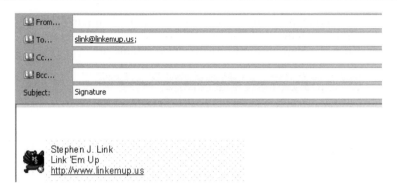

Figure 5-10 E-mail Signature

You can select and create a signature through the Tools–Options menu selections and then the Mail Format tab. The Signatures section is located at the bottom of that screen, as shown below.

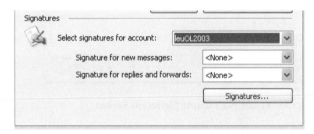

Figure 5-11 Selecting a Signature

You can create as many signatures as you want and assign separate signatures to each account you install.

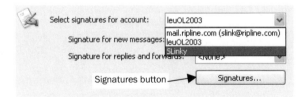

Figure 5-12 Selecting Multiple Signatures

If you click on the Signatures button (shown on the previous page), you will see the Create Signature screen. From here you can edit and remove signatures. Click the New button to create a new signature.

Figure 5-13 Create Signature Screen

The Create New Signature screen is shown on the following page. You can name the new signature and select how to begin. In addition to starting with a "blank screen", you can also base the new signature on an existing signature or template.

Figure 5-14 Creating a New Signature

As you can see, there are many different ways for you to format your signature.

Figure 5-15 Editing a Signature

Your can send your signature as a vCard attachment with each outgoing e-mail (see Figure 5-15 on the previous page).

A vCard is an attachment of the contact information associated with the selected contact record. Creating and saving a vCard is explained in the Contacts section under Creating a vCard from a Contact on page 8-39.

HTML Format

The best and most common e-mail format to use is HTML. If recipients are able to receive HTML e-mail, it will appear on their screens just as you designed it. Below you see the previous advertisement designed with WordMail and sent and received in HTML format.

Announcing
Link Em UP
On Outlook

If you need help on Outlook 2000, 2002, or 2003 we have a perfect resource for you. It is for the intermediate user.
That description should cover at least half of the Outlook user community.

It covers many features including the different types of accounts, contacts, and even Outlook Automation.

This could be just what you need to move your career to the next level.

Call 252-252-1234 to reserve your copy now.

Hurry!! Supplies are limited

Figure 5-16 HTML E-mail

Outlook Rich Text Format

It is possible that the recipient cannot receive HTML-formatted e-mail but can receive the RTF format. On the following page you'll see the same e-mail sent and received in Outlook Rich Text format.

Announcing
Link Em UP
On Outlook

If you need help on Outlook 2000, 2002, or 2003 we have a perfect resource for you. It is for the
intermediate user.
That description should cover at least half of the Outlook user community.

It covers many features including the different types of accounts, contacts, and even Outlook
Automation.

This could be just what you need to move your career to the next level.

Call 252-252-1234 to reserve your copy now.

Hurry!! Supplies are limited

Figure 5-17 RTF E-mail

Plain Text Format

One hideous possibility is that a recipient can only receive plain text. In
that case, no matter how hard you work on the e-mail, that person will
not be able to see anything other than plain, boring text. The publisher-
quality newsletter is pictured below in plain text.

```
Announcing

L i n k    E m    U p

On Outlook


If you need help on Outlook 2000, 2002, or 2003 we have a perfect resource for you.   It is for the intermediate user.

That description should cover at least half of the Outlook user community.


It covers many features including the different types of accounts, contacts, and even Outlook Automation.


This could be just what you need to move your career to the next level.

 |


Call 252-252-1234 to reserve your copy now.


Hurry!! Supplies are limited
```

Figure 5-18 Plain Text E-mail

Here's a "rule of thumb" you should always keep in mind when replying
to an e-mail:

➢   Always reply in the same format as the message was received

By following this rule, you'll know that the recipient will always be able to receive and view the e-mail as formatted. If you receive a message in HTML format, you know that the sender can view in HTML, so do not change the reply e-mail from that format.

➢ *Compose in this message format – HTML*	This is the best selection to be sure the e-mail recipient sees the e-mail as you composed it. Using this format, you can be quite elaborate in your e-mail formatting and rest assured that it will look the same on the recipient's screen as it does on yours.
➢ *Use Microsoft Word 2003 to edit e-mail messages* (checked)	This is another good option to select. It will help in formatting e-mails.

Configuring Views

These are some of the View options and the recommended settings for them. There are many others available. The premise to remember when changing Outlook settings is that you can't actually break it. If you don't like the effect of checking a box, just uncheck it.

View Definitions

➢ *View*	Views give you different ways to look at the same information in a folder by putting it in different arrangements and formats.
	There are standard views for each folder. (You can also create custom views.)
➢ *Navigation Pane*	This is the column on the left side of the Outlook window that includes panes such as Shortcuts or Mail and the shortcuts or folders within each pane.
	Click a folder to show the items in the folder.
➢ *Item*	An item is the basic element that holds information in Outlook (similar to a file in other programs).
	Items include e-mail messages, appointments, contacts, tasks, journal entries, notes, posted items, and documents.

> *Status bar* — A horizontal bar at the bottom of the screen that displays information about the current condition of the program, such as the status of items in the window, the progress of the current task, or information about the selected item.

> *Offline Folder files (.ost)* — The file on your hard disk that contains offline folders. The offline folder file has an .ost extension.

You can create it automatically when you set up Outlook or when you first make a folder available offline.

> *Fields* — An element of a table that contains a specific item of information, such as a last name.

A salutation field might contain "Mr." or "Ms." Databases such as Microsoft SQL Server refer to fields as columns. In simple terms, a field is a column heading.

> *View type* — The basic structure of a view.

When you create a view, you must first select one of five view types (table, timeline, day/week/month, card, or icon) to determine how information will be arranged and formatted in your new view.

> *Contact* — Person, inside or outside of your organization, about whom you can save several types of information, such as street and e-mail addresses, telephone and fax numbers, and Web page URLs.

> *Table* — A view type that displays a list of items (rows) and their attributes (columns).

Use this view to display details about items. Table is the default view type for Inbox and Tasks.

> *Shortcut group* — One of the groups of shortcuts to folders that can be displayed in the Shortcuts Pane.

> *Submenu* — A menu that appears when a user points to a command on a higher-level menu.

> *Column headings*   The horizontal bar at the top of one column in a table. There are multiple column headings in the column-heading row. Other programs might call this a field name.

Preview Messages

AutoPreview can be turned on or off. The views previously displayed have had AutoPreview turned off. The following image shows a view with it turned on.

Figure 5-19 Inbox with AutoPreview Turned on

The default view is for the Reading Pane (called the Preview Pane in previous versions) to be visible. With the Reading Pane turned on, there is no need to use AutoPreview. The Reading Pane is greatly improved over the Preview Pane in prior versions of Outlook. Instead of the preview displaying below the message, it can be read in a larger view to the right of the Inbox. If you prefer the Reading Pane to be at the bottom, it can be easily moved.

The Reading Pane may cause security concerns for some. If you are worried about a virus being sent through an email message and activated by the Reading Pane there is another option. Turn off the Reading Pane through the View menu (View – Reading Pane-Off).

If you would still like to use the Reading Pane but isolate your system from viruses as far as possible, the following changes can be made to Outlook:

1. Click on the Tools menu and then Options, Preferences tab, Email Options. Check Read All Standard Mail In Plain Text.

2. Click on the Tools menu and then Options, Security tab, Zone Settings (click OK on the message displayed). Change the Default Level to HIGH.

Three-pane View

A big improvement in Outlook 2003 over previous versions is the new three-pane view, shown below.

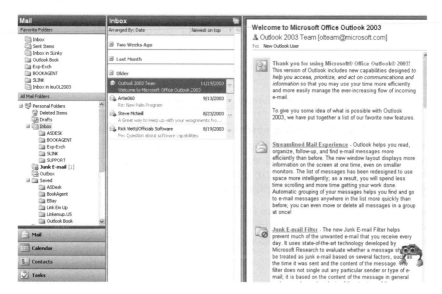

Figure 5-20 Three-pane View

As you can see, the amount of information seen in this view is quite extensive. "Upgraders" appreciate the visual improvements provided by the "pane" structure, and the ease of use:

> The Outlook Bar that used to run along the left side of the window has been replaced with the Navigation Pane. It combines the functionality of the old Outlook Bar with the old Folder List.

> The center pane is called the Inbox Pane. It displays all e-mails (with various sorting options) for the mailbox selected in the Navigation Pane.

> The right side of the graphic displays the Reading Pane. It is a tremendous improvement over the previously used Preview Pane.

Favorite Folders

One major improvement in Outlook 2003 is the Favorite Folders presentation. You can assign any folder to be included in your Favorite Folders listing.

Figure 5-21 Favorite Folders Listing

This view is now quite customized with the addition of four folders and the removal of many others, including Deleted Items. Notice the "Inbox in Slinky" and "Inbox in leuOL2003" entries. These are for Hotmail accounts. Yes, you can have multiple Hotmail accounts in Outlook 2003 (only one was permitted in the 2002 version).

Here is the complete Mail Folders tree. Notice that the Deleted Items folder is bolded and has a (1) beside it. This means that there is one message in the Deleted Items folder that has not been opened/read.

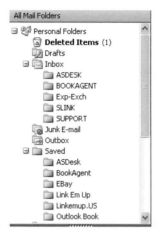

Figure 5-22 Mail Folders Tree

Grouping Messages

The sorting and grouping of messages is another nicely presented feature of Outlook 2003.

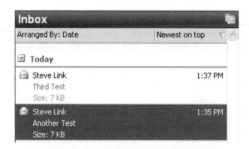

Figure 5-23 Sorting Messages by Date

You can view what came in for the past seven days (on a daily basis) and what is older. In the Figure above, there are three lines displayed with the size of the e-mail shown on the third line. These views are completely customizable.

The default types of e-mail groupings are:

➢ Date

➢ Conversation

> From
> To
> Folder
> Size (including attachment size)
> Subject
> Type
> Flag
> Attachments
> E-mail account
> Importance
> Categories

Choosing the option to display the messages in groups causes them to display according to the settings you create.

Customizing Settings

Customize the settings by right-clicking on the space below the last e-mail and selecting Customize Current View. You can also access this screen by clicking on View–Arrange By–Custom. The following dialog displays.

Figure 5-24 Customize Current View Screen

Field Settings

You can set whether the fields are displayed or hidden, how messages are grouped, sorted, filtered, along with other settings. Clicking on Fields displays the dialog box shown on the following page.

This dialog allows you to choose which fields are shown and the order in which they are listed. To add a field to the view, choose that field in the left-hand column and click the Add button.

To move that field up in the view order, choose it from the right column and click the Move Up button. Each click moves the field one level higher. Clicking on the Move Down button moves the selected field down one level. The levels actually appear from left to right when viewing message folders.

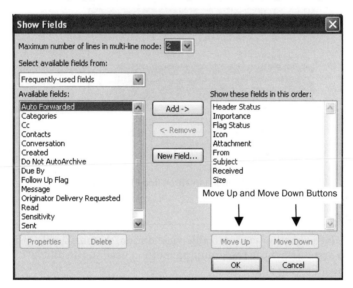

Figure 5-25 Show Fields Screen

At the top of this screen you'll see a setting for the maximum number of lines in the view. This controls the number of lines viewed in the folder view. The following graphic shows a two-line mode.

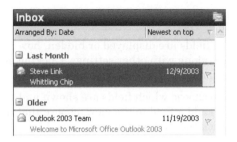

Figure 5-26 Inbox in Two-line Mode

This graphic displays a three-line mode:

Figure 5-27 Inbox in Three-line Mode

Group Settings

Grouping order is another customizable view option. Automatically group according to arrangement is the grouping method used in the dialog shown on the following page.

Figure 5-28 Automatic Grouping

You can also choose to use custom grouping. For instance, the graphic below shows Group items by To, Then by Subject. Notice that the Show Field In View option is unchecked for the To field. That is to say, you can use a field for grouping purposes even though you don't display it.

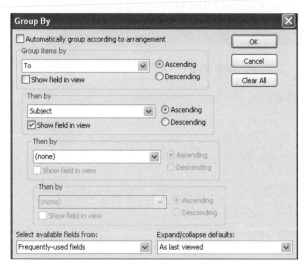

Figure 5-29 Custom Grouping

The messages in this grouping order display as follows:

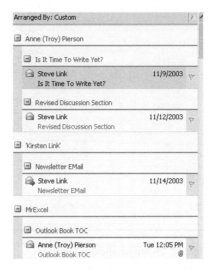

Figure 5-30 Message Displayed in Grouping Order

Setting Sort Order

The default sort order on the Inbox is received date.

Figure 5-31 Default Sort Order

You can change the sort order to any field you choose.

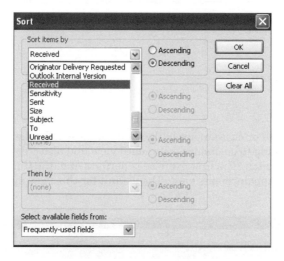

Figure 5-32 Changing Sort Order

The graphic below displays the Inbox sorted by Subject.

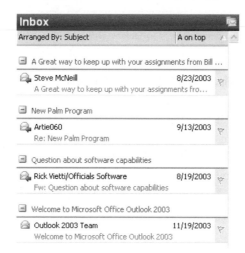

Figure 5-33 Inbox Sorted by Subject

Customizing Views

There are five basic types of views:

> Table

> Timeline

> Day/Week/Month

> Card

> Icon

All views (standard or custom) are built on one of these five views. In this section, we are going to customize a standard view and also create our own view from scratch. The first exercise is performed in the Calendar using the Active Appointments view. The default for this view appears as shown below.

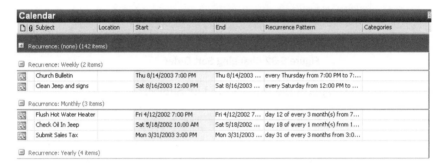

Figure 5-34 Default Calendar View

Customizing an Existing View

Now let's customize that view to show only those items that occur in the next week and are not in the Holiday category.

1. Right-click on an empty space in the calendar and left click on Customize Current View. The following screen appears.

Figure 5-35 Customizing the Current View

2. Click on the Filter button and then the Advanced tab.
3. Remove the default selection and create one for Start in the next 7 days. Set Categories to "doesn't contain Holiday". The screen should now look like the one shown below.

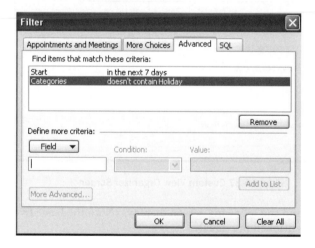

Figure 5-36 Filter, Advanced Tab Screen

4. Click OK.

The calendar now displays only those items that start in the next week and that exclude holidays. That was quite easy.

Customizing a View from Scratch

Now for the custom view from scratch. We are going use E-mail for this view and it have it display only those items received in the last three weeks that are flagged with the red or blue flags. We will also group by flags.

1. Click View–Arrange By–Current View–Define Views. The Custom View Organizer screen appears.

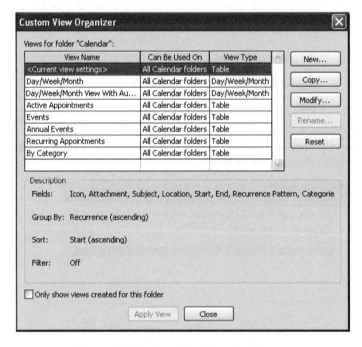

Figure 5-37 Custom View Organizer Screen

2. Click New and the following screen displays. Note the basic five view types we mentioned previously.

Figure 5-38 Creating a New View

3. We want to base the new view on the Table type and name it "Two week flagged". Click OK.

    The Customize View screen displays, as shown in Figure 5-35.

4. Click Filter. The Filter screen you see below comes up. Add the three filters shown in the Advanced tab.

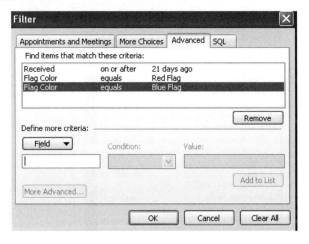

Figure 5-39 Filter, Advanced Tab Screen

5. Click OK and you are back to the Customize View screen. The next step is to apply the grouping specification.

6. Click on the Group By button, uncheck Automatically group... and choose Flag Status from the Group items by dropdown.

Figure 5-40 Group By Screen

7. Click OK. Notice in the following Figure that when this custom view is applied, only e-mail fitting the specified criteria is listed. Also notice the words "Filter Applied" in parentheses at the top right of this screen. It is now much easier to see when a filter is active.

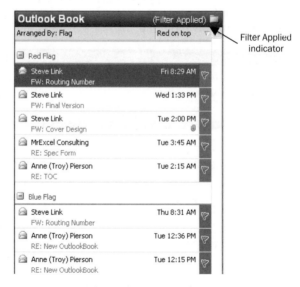

Figure 5-41 Inbox with Filter Applied

Setting E-mail Options

You can set up different E-mail options by clicking on the Tools–Options–Preferences menu option. See below for a partial screen shot.

Figure 5-42 Setting Preferences under Tools

Setting Junk E-mail Options

Clicking on the Junk E-Mail button displays the Junk E-Mail Options screen below. The greatly improved junk e-mail filtering in this version of Outlook could stand alone as the reason for upgrading!

You may want change the settings here to increase the amount of spam handled automatically. If you can't narrow down the list of safe senders for maximum spam protection, consider setting this option to High. You can retrieve any "false positives" with a quick review of the Junk E-mail folder.

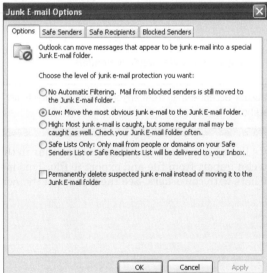

Figure 5-43 Setting Junk E-mail Options

Selecting Safe Senders, Safe Recipients, and Blocked Senders

Your settings can be as liberal as no automatic filtering at all (the top option) to only allowing mail from specific senders. You can define those specific senders by using the Safe Senders or Safe Recipients tab. Safe Senders appears below.

Figure 5-44 Selecting Safe Senders

Tip: You can automatically accept e-mail from anyone on your contacts list. Just click the bottom checkbox!

The Safe Recipients list appears and functions quite similar to this. On either of these you can import from file and export to file. This makes it easy to share your lists with coworkers. See the Figure on the next page.

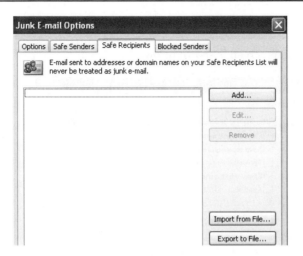

Figure 5-45 Selecting Safe Recipients

The Blocked Senders list is a nice feature for filtering junk e-mail. This list can contain either a specific address or an entire domain name. For instance, if you put @xyz.com in the list, all e-mail from that domain will be classified as junk e-mail.

Figure 5-46 Selecting Blocked Senders

Setting E-mail Options

The E-mail Options screen is shown below.

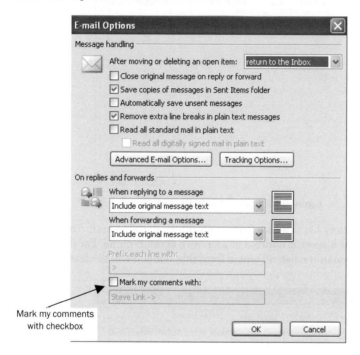

Mark my comments
with checkbox

Figure 5-47 Setting E-mail Options

Most options are self-explanatory. The Mark my comments with:
checkbox option provides a nice option to set apart text included in
replies and forwards.

Setting Advanced E-mail Options

The Advanced E-Mail Options appear on the following page. These
options let you tell Outlook which actions to take when new e-mail
arrives.

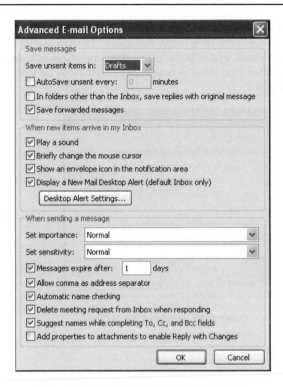

Figure 5-48 Setting Advanced E-mail Options

The default Display a New Mail Desktop Alert setting is another handy feature. The configuration screen for that is shown on the following page. A semi-transparent message appears on the upper right of your start bar and displays the title of the incoming e-mail.

Message desktop alerts only display for new, unread messages coming into the default account. They are triggered only during a normally scheduled send/receive and do not occur when a manual send/receive happens or during the initial synchronization when Outlook starts. Also note that rules can interfere with the desktop alert functionality.

Message Expiration settings and Suggesting names while typing the recipients are also a couple of interesting sending options you can use. Suggest Names can save you a lot of time when you address e-mail messages.

Let's set up a scenario where Message Expiration might be handy. You are planning a meeting at 11:00 tomorrow morning and are inviting twenty people. The message text indicates that they should respond by 10:30 a.m. so you will know how many to expect. In this case, a 10:30 expire time on the email would be helpful. If the message is received or not responded to after that time, a header will display to indicate that the message has expired.

Figure 5-49 Desktop Alert Settings

Setting Tracking Options

Let's take a quick look at the tracking options for a message.

A read receipt and delivery receipt can be requested for every e-mail you send out along with choosing how you handle them on your incoming e-mail. If you never want to send responses, you can handle that by choosing the Never send a response button near the bottom of this screen.

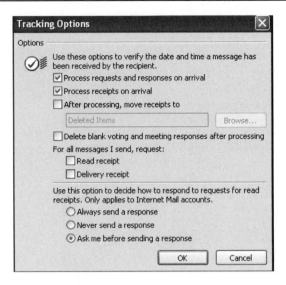

Figure 5-50 Setting Tracking Options

Creating a Custom Print Style

In this section we are going to create a custom print style. We will base it on the Table style and name it Table2.

1. Click File and then Print.
2. Click on the Table style and Define Styles.
3. Now click on the Copy button and name the new style Table2.

You can customize the format, fonts, header, footer, paper layout, and many other aspects. The average user will not generally need custom print styles, so we only mention it briefly here.

This page intentionally left blank.

6. Using Outlook 2003

Starting Out

Outlook 2003 offers many improvements and new features over the previous versions. Below you see the "introduction" e-mail you receive after installing Outlook 2003.

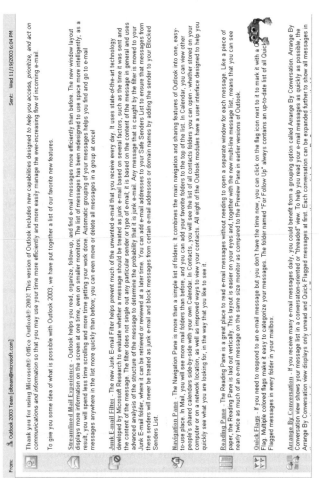

Figure 6-1 Outlook 2003 Introductory Message

Outlook Today

The first thing you see when starting the program is the new and improved Outlook Today.

Figure 6-2 Outlook Today Screen

You can customize Outlook using the Customize Outlook Today link in the upper right-hand corner (it could be located elsewhere, depending on the theme and format chosen). The aspects that you can customize in Outlook Today include which message folders to display, how many days of the calendar to display, which tasks to display, and the layout and style.

Configuring the "Classic" Interface

Let's suppose you dislike the "new and improved" appearance of Outlook 2003, but still enjoy the functionality it provides. Do you have to learn to live with the new interface? No.

In this section we will go through retrieving the old "look and feel" of the classic interface. Follow the steps below and you will come quite close to the old appearance.

Regaining the "Classic" Interface

1. Choose View–Arrange View–Current View–Define Views.
2. Select Messages, click Modify, and then click Other Settings.
3. Uncheck Show Items in groups.
4. Under Reading Pane, choose Bottom.

To make the Reading Pane take even less space, you can check Hide Header Information. Another option is to turn Reading Pane off completely and use Auto Preview instead.

5. Uncheck Use multi-line layout ... and check Always use single-line layout.

6. Click OK, make any desired changes to fields or other View settings, and click Apply View.

Unless views have been customized in other folders, this is the view you should see in all mail folders.

One advantage of the new Reading Pane layout being at the right side of the screen is that it allows for up to 40% more text to be shown, making scrolling less necessary.

Configuring Mail Grouping

Another advantage of the new interface is mail grouping. This makes viewing similar e-mails much easier. If the view is by date, the groups will be Today along with a daily listing back as far as a week. After that, the groups are two weeks, three weeks, one month, two months, and so on.

Groups include the following:

- ➢ Date
- ➢ Conversation
- ➢ From
- ➢ To
- ➢ Size
- ➢ Folder
- ➢ Subject

- ➢ Type
- ➢ Flag
- ➢ Attachments
- ➢ E-mail Account
- ➢ Importance
- ➢ Categories

Making Outlook the Default E-mail Client

When you install Outlook, set it to be the default e-mail client. This means that whenever you click an e-mail link on a web page link or choose Read Mail while browsing the web, Windows assigns Outlook to handle the task.

Making Outlook the Default E-mail Client – Again

The installation of certain programs can change the default e-mail client setting. Here, we'll cover how to change the setting for the default e-mail client back to Outlook.

1. Click on the Tools menu and then Options.
2. Click on the Other tab. The following dialog box displays.

Figure 6-3 Making Outlook the Default E-mail Program

This is the General section and is at the top of that screen.

3. Make sure that the "Make Outlook the default program for E-mail, Contacts, and Calendar" option is checked.

7. Organizing Outlook

Rules

You can use the rules in Outlook 2003 for spam filtering, automatic mail sorting, automatic mail forwarding, and many other things you may think of. In this section we will create a rule for automatically moving an incoming e-mail to a folder set up especially for it and create a rule that deletes all e-mail from a specific e-mail address.

Creating a New Rule

Both methods of creating a new rule (from a template and from a blank rule) are quite similar in procedure. We will cover the template approach here.

Moving Incoming E-mail to a Specified Folder

First, let's create that new folder.

1. Right-click on your Inbox and left-click on New Folder (see below).

Figure 7-1 Selecting New Folder from the Inbox

2. Name the new folder EBay. It will contain Mail and Post Items and will have e-mail from eBay® automatically directed to it.

Figure 7-2 Naming a New Folder

3. Now click on the Tools menu item and Rules and Alerts.

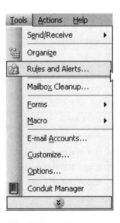

Figure 7-3 Selecting Rules and Alerts

4. Next, click on New Rule.

    We are going to create a rule to move an eBay incoming message to the folder we previously created.

Figure 7-4 Creating a New E-mail Rule

5. Left-click on Move messages with specific words..., and then click Next.

Figure 7-5 Rules Wizard Start up Screen

6. The Rules Wizard Set up screen displays. Notice that the option you want is already checked in the top box because of the selection you made in Step 5 above.

7. Now you need to left-click on the "specific words" link under Step 2: Edit the rule description to bring up the Search Text box.

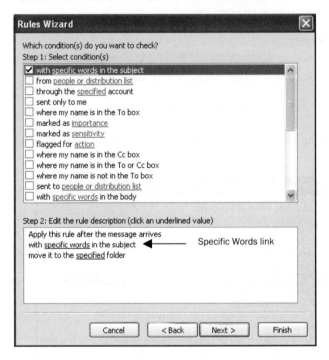

Figure 7-6 Rules Wizard Set up Screen

8. Enter EBay (see next page) and click the Add button. This results in moving any new e-mail containing the word "eBay" to the specified folder.

   This is a broad rule, but you can make it as specific as you want. You could create multiple folders, let's say eBay Questions, eBay Sold, and eBay Purchased, and use different rules to automatically move incoming messages into the appropriate folder.

Tip: It's a good idea to include possible variations in spelling or capitalization of the word that you are looking for.

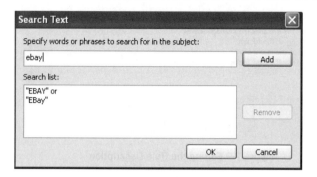

Figure 7-7 Specifying Text for Search

9. The next step is to click on the "specified folder" link, also under Step 2. The Rules and Alerts screen displays, similar to the one below.

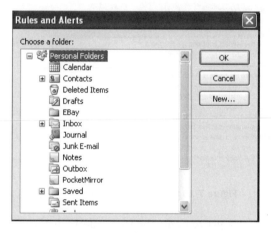

Figure 7-8 Choosing a Folder

10. Left-click on the eBay folder and click on the OK button. Now the box in Step 2 looks like the screen following screen. Click on Next twice.

Figure 7-9 Editing the Rule Description

11. This is the point where you can add exceptions if you want to. Exceptions allow you to greatly customize this rule in the hopes that you have "covered all of the bases." We will save exceptions for later. Click Next.

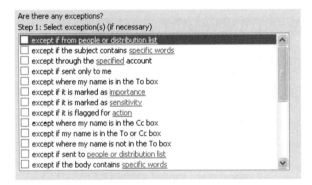

Figure 7-10 Selecting Exceptions

12. In the final step, you get to name the rule, select whether to run it now, select whether to turn it on, and do a final review and edit of the rule itself. Click Finish when you're done. You have now created a rule from a template.

Figure 7-11 Finishing Rule Setup

Deleting a Message from a Specific Address

Next, we are going to create a second rule, one that deletes a message from a specific address. Let's say that you want to delete all e-mail from spamsender@mrspam.edu. Our new rule will handle that.

1. Start by clicking on Tools and then Rules and Alerts. The same Rules Wizard screen you saw previously displays. Click New Rule, then Start creating a rule from a template.

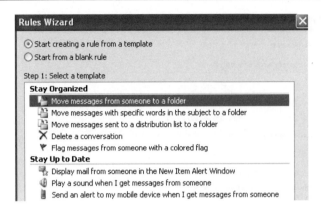

Figure 7-12 Rules Wizard Start up Screen

2. The first selection here is Move messages from someone to a folder.
   That is the template we'll use for this application. Click Next.

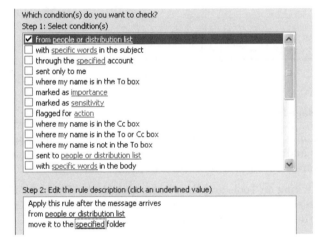

Figure 7-13 Rules Wizard Set up Screen

3. As before, the proper option is already selected. Now you'll enter the
   e-mail address to be used. Click on the "people or distribution list"
   link (underlined in blue in Step 2 above) so you can enter the
   contacts.

4. You can select an address from the contacts list or enter it manually.
   This is a spammer's address, so you will need to enter it manually.

Locate the From field at the bottom of this screen and type the address there. Click OK and then Next.

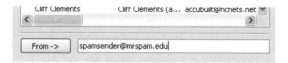

Figure 7-14 Entering the "From" Address

Notice that the proper action is selected again.

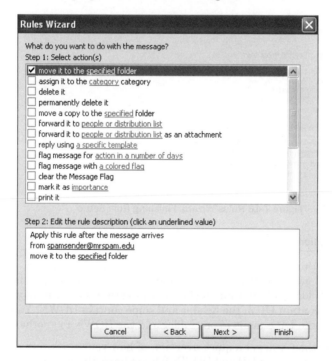

Figure 7-15 Rules Wizard Set up Screen

5. Now you need to select the folder to which the e-mails will be moved. Click on the specified link (underlined in blue in Step 2) and select Deleted Items from the folder tree. Click OK and then Next.

6. The next step is to set up exceptions. If this rule was set to delete all messages from @mrspam.edu, but you knew Bob at that location and still wanted to receive his e-mail, you could put his address in as an

Exception. Since this is only a single e-mail address, there are no exceptions to set. Click Next.

7. The final step is to name the rule and decide when it will be run, turned on, and so forth. You can also review the rule and make any modifications you may have forgotten when you were breezing through the wizard. Click on any of the links to make these changes. Click Finish when the rule has been verified. You're done!

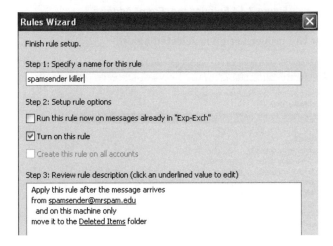

Figure 7-16 Rules Wizard, Finishing Rule Setup

Applying Exceptions

Let's create a third rule and add exceptions to this one. Here is the scenario – you own ten different stocks and get twenty e-mails per day (mid-day and closing) from your stockbroker updating the status of your stocks. Some contain UP in the header and some contain DOWN. You want to move the UP e-mails to one folder and the DOWN to another.

Using this method, you get a quick overview of how your stocks are doing. We will assume that the UP and DOWN folders have already been created. This function requires two rules – one to move messages into the UP folder and another to move them into the DOWN folder.

1. As you did before, click on Tools and Rules and Alerts. You will see the beginning rules screen. We will also create this rule from a template.

2. Click on the New Rule button. Verify that the Start creating a rule from a template button is selected and click on the Move messages with specific words in the subject to a folder selection. Click Next.

3. In this rule we are selecting two conditions to work with – e-mail from a specific address and e-mail containing specific words in the subject. Both of these boxes should be checked as illustrated below.

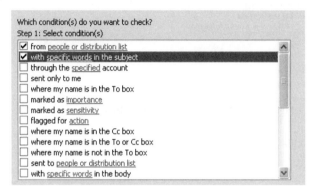

Figure 7-17 Rules Wizard Set up Screen

4. Under Step 2, click on the "specific words" link, and then type UP. Click Add and then OK.

5. Click on the people or distribution list link and type bob@linkemup.us in the FROM field as illustrated below. Click OK and then Next.

Figure 7-18 Rules Wizard, Entering "From" Address

6. Now verify that the Move it to a specified folder selection is checked and click on the specified link under Step 2 of this section. Select the UP folder from the folder list and click on the OK button. Click Next.

7. Now we are at the Exceptions screen. You also receive new stock tips from Bob. Since you are not really interested in new stocks, these messages should be deleted. Check the Except if the subject contains specific words selection and then click on the specific words link in Step 2 of this section.

8. In the Search Text screen, type in New Stock. Click Add and then OK. Click Next to proceed to naming the rule.

9. Name the rule "Stock Up" and review it on this screen. The rule created here should appear as it does in the following screen.

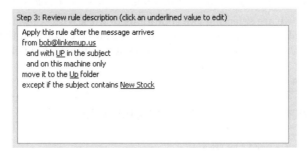

Figure 7-19 Rules Wizard, Finishing Rule Set up

10. After verifying the rule procedures, click Finish.

Making a Copy

As you know, we want two rules that perform almost the exact same functionality (Stock Up and Stock Down). Therefore, we need to create another rule. We can either go through the steps to create a new rule or we can use the Copy Rule button to simplify the process.

1. The main rule screen should now be displayed with the rules listed. Select the rule you just created and named Stock Up (it should be on top) and click on the Copy Rule button (third from left) as illustrated below.

Figure 7-20 Copying a Rule

2. Select the destination for the rule. Most people will have only one Inbox and that will automatically be selected. Click OK.

3. Now a rule appears at the bottom of the list called Copy of Stock Up. Click that and click the Change Rule button. The Change Rule menu is illustrated in the following Figure.

Figure 7-21 Changing a Rule

4. First we want to rename the rule to Stock Down. Click on Rename Rule; type in Stock Down and click OK.

5. Click on Change Rule once more and then on Edit Rule Settings. You will see the rule settings laid out in the Step 2 box as before. We only need to make two changes, both in this section.

6. Click on the first UP link (as shown in the Step 3 box in Figure 7-19). Click the word Up in the box and click the Remove button. Type in Down and click the Add button.

7. Next click the Up folder link and select Down from the folder list that displays. Click OK. Verify that the rule appears as shown below and click Finish to complete the process.

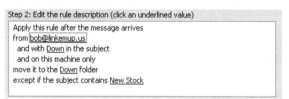

Figure 7-22 Editing a Rule Description

8. The final step in this process is to turn the rule on. You may also want to move it up in the order of processing. To activate the rule, make sure that box on the left side of it is checked.

Changing a Rule's Processing Order

You may also want to move the rule up or down in the order of processing. You can do this using the Up and Down arrows above the rules listing. Select a rule and click on the appropriate arrow to move that rule to the desired position.

Figure 7-23 Changing a Rule's Processing Order

In this section we have created several rules. It is important to note that you can create as many rules as you desire. Keep in mind, though, that the more rules being processed for every message means a longer time before you receive your messages. The order of rules is also quite important. Of course, the specific order of rules depends on each individual circumstance; there is no "set in stone" order for rules.

Another point to keep in mind is junk e-mail rules. These are also processed for each incoming e-mail.

There are a couple more buttons that need to be mentioned here.

Deleting a Rule

To delete a rule, select the rule you want to delete and then click the Delete button above the rules listing. This permanently removes the rule. If you want to keep the rule around to possibly turn it on later, you can uncheck the rule. If you uncheck a rule, it will not run but you can still turn it on later if want to without the bother of recreating it.

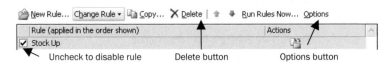

Figure 7-24 Deleting a Rule

Rule Options Button

This button is also above the rules listing (see Figure above). Clicking on it displays the Options screen.

Figure 7-25 Rules Options

Using this, you can easily export rules to other computers or import them from other systems. You can also upgrade your rules. The Upgrade Now button will not be available if Outlook 2003 was installed fresh or if there were no rules in the version from which it was upgraded.

Import and Export Rules are quite basic in functionality in so far as there are *no safety prompts.* It is very easy to inadvertently double up on the rules by clicking on Import and choosing to load a second set of rules.

> Tip: Be sure to exercise caution when deleting rules. When a rule is deleted, the selector bar moves to the rule above it. If you are deleting a second set of rules, start at the bottom rule and work up to the first "extra" rule.

Using Find

The Find option under the Tools menu allows you to search through your e-mail, contacts, appointments, and so forth. You type in the text to search for, choose where to search, and then select other options.

Making a Simple Search

Follow the steps below to make a simple text search within a folder.

1. Select Tools–Find–Find. The Find bar displays. See the Figure on the following page.

Figure 7-26 Find Bar

2. Type the string to search for in the Look for box.

3. Select the location where you want to search using the Search In dropdown box.

Figure 7-27 Search In Drop Down Box

4. Click Find Now.

Making an Advanced Search

Notice that there is an Options box on the far right of the Find bar (see Figure 7-26 above). Click on it to select Advanced Find. As you can see in Figure 7-28, Advanced Find gives you many more options for searching through your Outlook items. You can set these options to progressively narrow your search.

In the Look For dropdown, you have the following options:

> Any type of Outlook item

> Appointments and Meetings

> Contacts

> Files

> Journal Entries

> Messages

> Notes

> Tasks

To look for text anywhere within Outlook, choose any type of Outlook item. To narrow the search area, you can choose a specific type of item, such as Messages in the following Figure.

Messages Tab

Under the Messages tab, enter the words or phrase you want to search for along with the field in which to search. Use the Browse button to select the desired location. You can also select a location from the Find bar (see Figure 7-26).

These are the fields you can choose from to narrow the search:

> Subject field only
> Subject field and message body
> Frequently used text fields

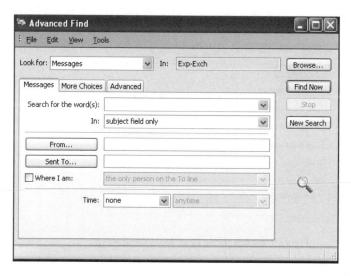

Figure 7-28 Advanced Find, Messages Tab

The section below that, which has From and Sent To, lets you narrow the search tremendously. By choosing whom the message is from, to whom it was sent, and/or choosing Where I am (your e-mail address will be in the To or CC field), you can narrow the search field to only a few messages.

If you know when the message was sent, received, expired, etc., you can use the Time option to narrow the search field even more. The selections for Time are none, received, sent, due expires, created, and modified. The selections for the anytime field are yesterday, today, in the last seven days, last week, this week, last month, and this month.

More Choices Tab

On the More Choices tab (center tab), you have these additional choices for finding items.

> Specific categories for the retrieved item

> Only items that are either read or unread

> Only items with no attachments or one or more attachments

> Items whose importance is Normal, High, or Low

> Only items which have no flag or a specific color flag

> Match case

> A size that is equal to, between, less than, or greater than entered values

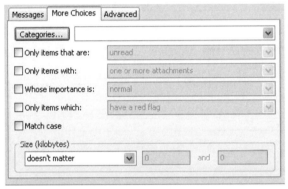

Figure 7-29 Advanced Find, More Choices Tab

Advanced Tab

On the Advanced tab, you have an opportunity to specify which field(s) contain, don't contain, or are equal to the value entered. The other two options here are "is empty" and "is not empty". When you have selected the criteria in this tab, click Add To List.

Although there is no limit to the number of criteria that you can enter for a Find, restraint still has to be exercised in their use. Too many criteria can so finely restrict the Find that nothing will display!

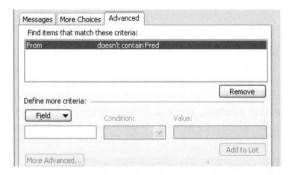

Figure 7-30 Advanced Find, Advanced Tab

Filtering

Filtering is an extremely useful—and bothersome, at times—option. The reason filtering can be highly bothersome is that we can easily forget that a filter is in place. This seems to be the cause for the mysterious disappearance of e-mail messages for many users. Clearing the filter settings clears up the problem.

To access Filtering, right-click on the space below the last e-mail and select Customize Current view and then select Filter from the Customize View: Messages screen.

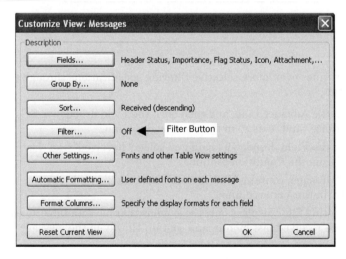

Figure 7-31 Customize Current View Screen

Messages Tab

If you have an Inbox with hundreds of e-mails and want to view ONLY the mail from a certain person, you would use filtering. The Filter screen's Message tab is nearly identical to that of the Advanced Find screen (see Figure 7-28). On the Messages tab, you can filter for specific word(s) in a particular location. You can further filter based on who sent a message (From), To whom it was sent, Where your address appears, and the Time.

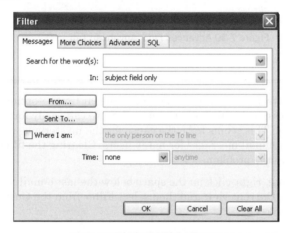

Figure 7-32 Filter, Messages Tab

Advanced Tab

Filtering provides even more selective filtering specifications through the Advanced tab.

1. Click on the Advanced tab, and then click the Field dropdown. Select "Importance" and "exists" in the Condition column.

2. Click on the Field dropdown again and select "Received" and "last month" from the Condition column.

3. Select "Message, contains" in the Condition column, and type "Howdy" in the Value column.

   The resulting filter displays only those items that have an Importance flag, were received last month, and contain Howdy in the message.

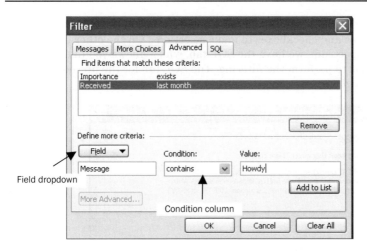

Figure 7-33 Configuring an Advanced Filter

There are many fields from which to choose in the Field dropdown.
Format Columns, the last item on the Customize View screen (shown in
Figure 7-31, also has many options and settings. See the following
Figure.

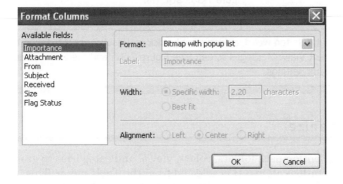

Figure 7-34 Filter, Format Columns

Note that only the From, Subject, Received, and Size fields allow the
selection of Label, Width, and Alignment (grayed out above). The other
two tabs – More Choices and SQL – are only mentioned briefly here
because their functionality is duplicated in the Advanced tab.

More Choices gives you a limited, but simpler, method of setting filters drop down boxes and checkboxes to make selections. On the other end of the difficulty spectrum, we have the SQL tab, which allows you to use SQL commands to perform the filtering. The SQL tab for the preceding filter appears below.

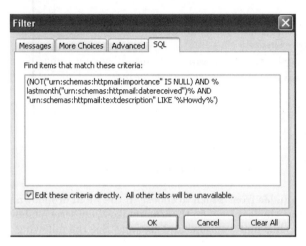

Figure 7-35 - SQL Tab

Tip: If the layout gets too weird looking, simply click on Reset Current View on the Customize Current View: Messages screen (see Figure 7-31) and the view will go back to the default settings.

Using Organize

The Organize option uses folders, colors, views, and categories to group and/or move Outlook items. It is selected from the Tools menu. This feature is available for all areas within Outlook, but different types of items will only use certain methods of organization.

For instance, the organize option in mail uses folders, colors, and views, but only categories and views are available for organizing the calendar items. See the following page for an explanation of the main Organize screens.

Figure 7-36 Organize Screen – Using Folders

These are the options that you can use to organize your e-mail. First, select the e-mail(s) to which these settings will be applied. Your three options are explained below.

> Using Folders   Selected message(s) are moved to the chosen folder

> This is a one-time procedure and does not affect any messages that arrive later.

> Using Colors   Applies a chosen color to messages to or from a specific address

> You can also show messages sent ONLY TO ME in a specific color. As with Using Folders, Using Colors applies only to messages currently in the inbox and does not affect future arrivals.

> Using Views   Lets you choose different views (last seven days, sent to, message timeline, and others).

> This affects only the way messages are viewed.

These three options only affect the mail already received. To change the behavior of e-mail arriving in the future, you would use Rules and Alerts. Rules will automatically delete, move, or color (or just about any other action you can imagine) an incoming message. Rules are explained in great detail in Chapter 7, Organizing Outlook, Rules section on page 7-1.

This page intentionally left blank.

8. Outlook Folders

This section discusses the folders available to you in Outlook. These include the Calendar, Research, Contacts, Deleted Items, Drafts, Journal, Notes, Outbox, Sent Items, and Tasks. This is a lot of information to cover, so take a deep breath. Don't be afraid – it doesn't bite.

Using Subfolders

Before we get deeply into Outlook's folders, let's take a quick look at how to use its subfolders. As illustrated below, any Outlook folder can be organized with sub-folders. These sub-folders contain the same type of objects as the parent folder (here SLINK is a sub-folder of the Inbox folder, so it contains Mail items).

Figure 8-1 All Mail Folders with Subfolders

To create a sub-folder, right-click on the folder under which you want your sub-folder and then select New Folder from the drop-down menu.

Figure 8-2 Right-click Folder Options

The screen to create a new folder is displayed below.

Figure 8-3 Create New Folder Screen

Type in the name of the new folder; select which type of items it contains and where the folder resides. Below is the list of possible item contents for the new folder.

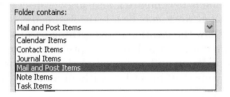

Figure 8-4 List of Item Contents for New Folder

If you are creating a new Inbox subfolder, it will contain Mail and Post items. A Contacts sub-folder contains Contact items. The Inbox examples show five sub-folders. You can manually move messages into these subfolders after you review them or have them moved automatically (based on sender, subject, etc.) using rules. There is a thorough explanation of rules in Chapter 7, Organizing Outlook, in the Rules section on page 7-1.

The depth of subfolders is virtually unlimited. For example, you could have a folder structure similar to the one illustrated below.

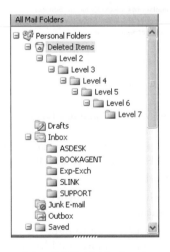

Figure 8-5 Subfolder Levels

There are seven levels below the Deleted Items folder. The chance of properly utilizing levels this deep is quite slim. Exercise caution when creating subfolders. A couple of levels deep can be easily used and helpful in maintaining proper organization. More than that (as illustrated here) could cause confusion.

An effective visualization is to compare a four-drawer desk with a typical roll top desk. Your desk at work may be a little cramped on space, but it is organized and you know the location of everything because there are only four drawers to hold it all. A roll top desk provides many more opportunities for classification and organization, but it also provides many more places for your stuff to get lost without an effective system.

Here's another reason for caution drawn from the previous example. Let's say that you are out sick one day and your boss needs to find something in your desk. Which of these methods will be easier for him to use and more convenient—fifty drawers or four neatly organized drawers? Four, of course.

Calendar Folder

Organizing Your Calendar

Figure 8-6 Ways to Organize a Calendar

Outlook provides two basic options you can use to organize your calendar. These options are explained below. First, select the appointment(s) to which these settings will be applied.

> Using Categories Adds the chosen category to all selected appointments

This method is quite handy if you imported some contacts from another address book. Select all of those contacts and use Organize to assign a category to them.

➢ Using Views   Changes the way the items are viewed but does not change any aspect of the entry itself

This method has the same functionality in all of the different items.

Although the organize functionality is available in all of the other items, the four basic tasks (mail, calendar, contacts, and items) are the same as already explained. Because of this, you are left to explore these on your own.

Setting Up the Microsoft Free/Busy Service

You will need a ".Net" account in order to use this service. The .Net account is free and so is the service, so follow the procedures below and enjoy!

The screen shot shown below lists the various Free/Busy options along with selections for setting up your own Free/Busy access page.

1. Click Tools–Options–Calendar Options, and then click Free/busy Options.
2. Check the Publish and search ... box and then click on Manage to set up your Free/Busy account. You will be prompted to set up a .Net account if you do not have one already.

> Tip: If necessary, type in name of the server where you will store your free/busy information in the Publish at this URL box. Publishing free/busy information at your own server would make it necessary to type in a URL. Also, if you are using the standard free/busy service, it is unnecessary to type anything because the location is already known. You can specify a default server in the Search at this URL box. You may need to contact your ISP provider for this information. The file extension for free/busy files is .vfb.

3. The default web browser starts up with the .Net login page. Login properly and click OK. The screen you use to invite members to view your calendar is shown on the following page. It appears as soon as you log in.

Authorize access and invite nonmembers to join

Add people to the list of authorized users who can view your free/busy times. (To view a list of all users you've authorized so far, in the navigation bar on the left, click **View my authorized users**.)

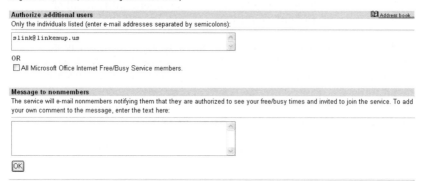

Figure 8-7 Authorizing Access to Your Calendar

4. Click OK to invite the member(s) listed.

The Free/Busy options are shown in the following screen.

> Select Publish At My Location if your own server will be hosting the free/busy info.

> Request free/busy tells Outlook to ask for authorization to view a user's calendar (when scheduling a meeting) if that authorization has not already been granted.

> Use Search Location to tell Outlook where to look for other user's free/busy information if you are publishing to a user-specified location.

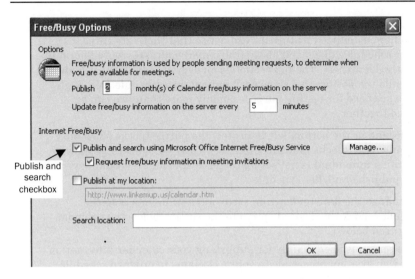

Figure 8-8 Free/Busy Options

5. Indicate how often you want Outlook to update your free/busy information on the server and how many months of your data you want available.

6. After signing up for a .NET account and checking the Publish and search checkbox shown above, click OK.

7. To initiate the publishing procedure, you need to click on Tools–Send/Receive–Free/Busy Information. This publishes your calendar on the Free/Busy server, making it available for viewing by those to whom you granted access.

    Busy times from the Free/Busy service appear similar to the screen shot below.

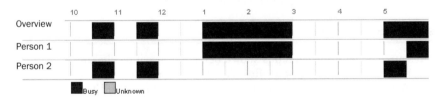

Figure 8-9 Free/Busy Chart

Notice that an eight-hour time slot is shown. This cannot be changed in the Free/Busy service (of course, using Exchange Server or one of the other calendar sharing programs or services allows access to this and many other customized features). Also notice that there are three different schedules displayed above (the e-mail addresses were left off to protect the identities). The top section is an overview of all the schedules listed while the bottom two show each individual's schedule. Although only two are used for testing purposes, many more than two can be displayed together.

As the legend at the bottom left indicates, the purple blocks show busy times while gray blocks indicate Unknown. Gray will generally show if the specified individual is not set up correctly for the Free/Busy service or has not published his/her schedule.

8. To change the date and/or time or to add new members to the calendar, click the desired option in the section below the calendar (pictured below).

    This screen is used mainly for publishing your calendar information to a web location accessible to your associates in order to schedule meetings and resources.

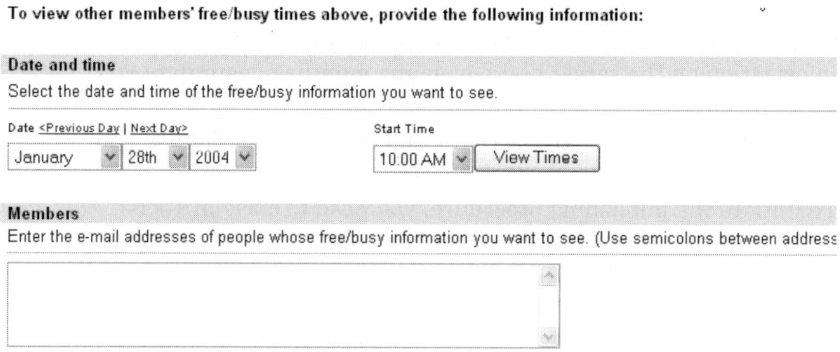

To view other members' free/busy times above, provide the following information:

Date and time

Select the date and time of the free/busy information you want to see.

Date <u><Previous Day</u> | <u>Next Day></u>   Start Time

| January ⌄ | 28th ⌄ | 2004 ⌄ | | 10.00 AM ⌄ | View Times |

Members

Enter the e-mail addresses of people whose free/busy information you want to see. (Use semicolons between address

Figure 8-10 Changing Date/Time and Adding New Members

Resource Scheduling

The Resource Scheduling screen is shown below. Access if by clicking Tools–Options–Calendar Options–Resource Scheduling. Resource Scheduling is used in conjunction with Exchange Server. Since Exchange Server is not the focus of this book, we will only give brief explanations of a few options here.

These are your options for responding to meeting requests: Note that the bottom two choices are not available unless the Automatically Accept ... box is checked.

➢ Automatically accept meeting requests and process cancellations
   If a user includes you in a meeting and the time is open on your calendar it will be automatically accepted. Cancellations are automatically removed from your calendar with this option checked also.

➢ Automatically decline conflicting meeting requests
   Declines a meeting request if that time slot is already occupied on your calendar.

➢ Automatically decline recurring meeting requests
   No recurring meeting requests will be allowed through. They are automatically rejected.

Figure 8-11 Scheduling Resources

Time Zone Settings

Time zone settings are a big issue in using Outlook, especially if you are e-mailing (or scheduling) resources that may be located in another time zone. Those options are shown in the following figure.

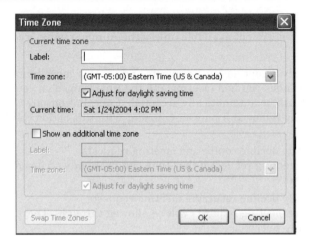

Figure 8-12 Time Zone Screen

It is quite important to have your time zone settings correct. If they are not, the results could be as minor as times being off on e-mail or as major as scheduling a meeting time for 11 a.m. when you intended it to be 2 p.m. (Pacific time zone versus Eastern).

All time-based functions (e-mail, meetings, and so forth) are affected by the time zone settings for both the sender and the recipient(s).

Label is a user-defined label that you can assign to a time zone. For example, the time zone shown here is Eastern; you could assign it the label EST.

If you want to view a second time zone (perhaps a time zone you travel to often) click Show an additional time zone. The Swap Time Zones button becomes available. Clicking this will show your appointments as if they were in that time zone.

Adding Holidays

Clicking on the Add Holidays button displays the screen below.

Figure 8-13 Add Holidays

Selecting the appropriate country and clicking on OK adds these holidays to your calendar automatically. The screen shot below shows how Christmas (U.S. holiday) appears in the calendar.

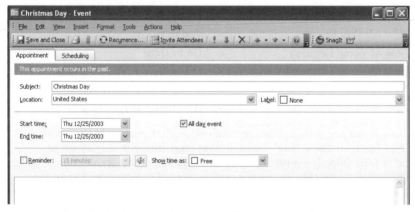

Figure 8-14 Christmas Day Automatically Placed on Calendar

Holidays are automatically assigned to the Holiday category. They are added as all day events but are not set to be recurring.

Setting Planner Options

Here are the Planner Options. Use these options when you want to
schedule meetings or group events.

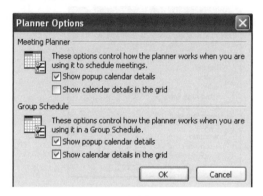

Figure 8-15 Planner Options

Calendar Right-click Menu

The right-click menu for a calendar item lists the following items:

- New Appointment
- New All Day Event
- New Meeting Request
- New Meeting Request With
- New Recurring Appointment
- New Recurring Event

- New Recurring Meeting
- Today
- Go to Date
- Other Settings
- Customize Current View
- Automatic Formatting

The New items are self-explanatory. An option that makes things easier
is the addition of "Recurring" for each item (appointment, all day event,
and so on). By selecting a recurring option, you can create a calendar
item beginning with the recurrence screen instead of having to remember
to click on the Recurrence button after you create the appointment.

The Today and Go to Date options move to either the current date or the
selected date.

Other Settings, Customize Current View, and Automatic Formatting are
covered in detail in other chapters (see Customizing Settings on page 5-
24, Customizing Views on page 5-30, Regaining the "Classic" Interface on
page 6-2, and Calendar Right-click Menu on page 8-12).

Side-by-Side Calendar View

One of the Calendar features new to Outlook 2003 is the side-by-side calendar view as shown in the following figure.

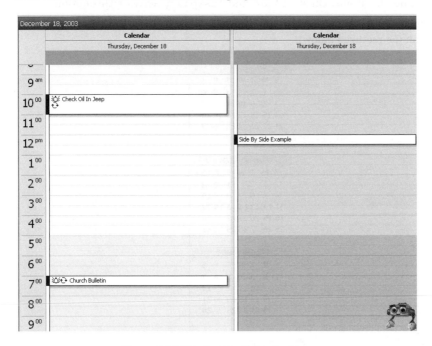

Figure 8-16 Side-by-Side Calendar View

In the Navigation Pane, click on Calendar. Now look in the My Calendars section to the left. There you see your personal calendar listed along with any other calendar folders in your mailbox, active personal folders files, and Exchange Server (if applicable). Click the check box beside any of these calendars to display them side-by-side.

The application possibilities here are tremendous. If you are trying to set up a meeting with three other people and you have access to their calendars, you can view them all at once to choose the best meeting time.

Using Taskpad

If you actively use tasks, you may find it helpful to see them listed along with calendar items. Click on View and Taskpad to activate this option.

With the Taskpad view active, the calendar days move to the Taskpad section (as pictured below).

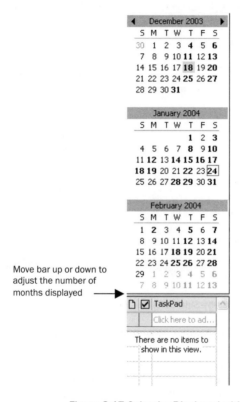

Move bar up or down to adjust the number of months displayed ⟶

Figure 8-17 Calendar Displayed with Taskpad

By placing the mouse cursor on the bar at the bottom of the calendar, you can increase or decrease the number of months viewed by moving the bar up or down.

Sending Meeting Requests

An Exchange Server is not required for sending a meeting request, although it makes management of the requests much more efficient. You can send a meeting request over the Internet to someone who is using Outlook 2002 and above. This section takes you through the procedure to send an Internet meeting request.

1. Click on the arrow beside New and select Meeting Request. A screen similar to the one shown below appears.

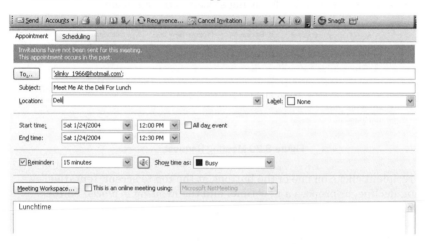

Figure 8-18 Meeting Request Screen

2. Click on the Scheduling tab to view a Scheduling screen similar to the following figure.

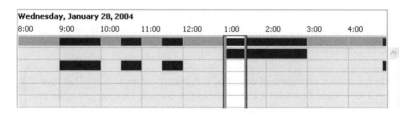

Figure 8-19 Scheduling Screen

This screen uses Exchange Server if it is present. It also utilizes the Microsoft Free/Busy service to let you view your busy times if you have signed up for it.

3. With the ability to view an invitee's schedule, you have the opportunity to choose an open time and schedule an activity.

    At the bottom of the scheduling screen, you can change the meeting date and time in case one of the attendees is unavailable during the originally chosen time.

    When you send out a meeting request for a scheduled activity, it looks something like the following screen to the recipient.

Figure 8-20 Meeting Request

The recipient clicks on one of the buttons at the top to accept, tentatively accept, decline, or propose a new time, and the meeting is placed on the recipient's calendar.

Forward Your Calendar as iCalendar

Calendar sharing is discussed in detail in another section of this chapter (see Setting Up the Microsoft Free/Busy Service on page 8-5 and Resource Scheduling on page 8-8. One of the simpler methods of sharing is to forward the calendar item as an iCalendar.

The biggest problem with this method is that updating an item does not update it for all recipients automatically. You have to manually forward it to all of the recipients with every change.

> Note: Outlook provides no means of detecting a duplicate calendar item. That is, if you receive a forwarded item with a change from the original, Outlook just adds that item to your calendar. If you receive a replacement calendar item, you need to manually delete the original.

Setting Calendar Options

To set up different calendar options, click on the Tools–Options and select the Preferences tab. The following Figure shows a partial screen shot of what you should see.

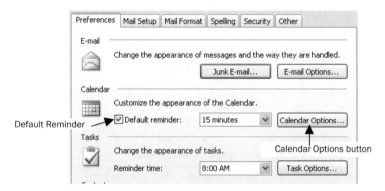

Figure 8-21 Preferences Tab, Default Calendar Reminder

You can set the default reminder from 0 minutes to two weeks.

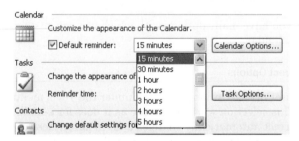

Figure 8-22 Setting Default Calendar Reminder

Clicking on the Calendar Options button displays the following screen.

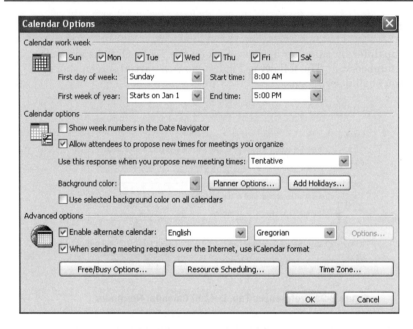

Figure 8-23 Calendar Options Screen

As you can see, you have many options with which you can customize your use of the calendar.

Calendar AutoCorrect Options

You'll find an AutoCorrect Options selection under the Tools menu for a calendar item. This selection works the same as it does for e-mail. For example, autocorrect automatically changes a "c" in parentheses (c) to a copyright symbol © and corrects common misspellings, such as replacing "accidant" with "accident".

You can customize the types of corrections to be made along with the list of misspellings to fit your own style. See the following screen shot.

Figure 8-24 Configuring AutoCorrect Options

You can tailor the autocorrect options to fit your particular typing quirks. For instance, if you are prone to type TO PEOPLE instead of TWO PEOPLE, you can add these phrases to the Replace and With boxes.

Another excellent time saver is the ability to replace a few letters with an entire phrase. To coin a common Internet shortcut, if you commonly use the abbreviation "rotfl" to indicate rolling on the floor laughing in e-mail, you could use autocorrect to replace "rotfl" with the words "rolling on the floor laughing".

Setting Calendar Views

If you are running an upgrade from another version of Outlook, the improved two-pane calendar view is a new feature that should receive many kudos. Notice in the following the screen shots that the left pane is neatly organized with the current month and the next month displayed for easy navigation.

Also, notice the full day view with each item in its specific time slot. Concurrent appointments are handled extremely well in this version. If you start to schedule an appointment close to another one, a warning displays on the screen. Notice that there are three appointments all scheduled at noon in this screen shot. They are all easily viewable and accessible.

There are four different calendar views—day, week, workweek, and month—shown on this and the following page. Notice that the date range shown is also highlighted in yellow in the left pane.

Each view has a different application and purpose. The daily view is most useful in scheduling and reviewing your entire day while the week and workweek views give a brief overview of what is planned for the week. The latter two would not seem as functional for planning the busy weekdays.

The month view is very brief in the detail displayed. It should work quite well for scheduling something during a light day instead of a busy day.

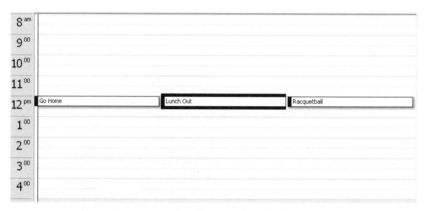

Figure 8-25 Calendar in Daily View with Simultaneous Events

Figure 8-26 Calendar in Weekly View

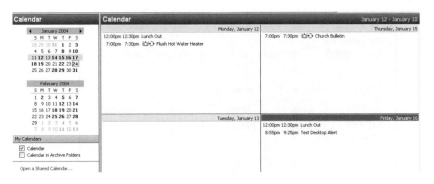

Figure 8-27 Calendar in Workweek View

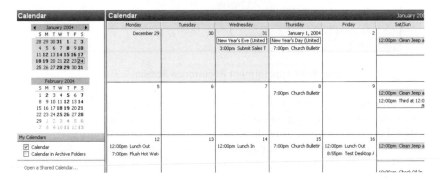

Figure 8-28 Calendar in Monthly View

Recurring Appointments

The Appointment Recurrence screen lets you verify your start and end times along with the duration. You can also choose the recurrence pattern (daily, weekly, monthly, or yearly) along with when to reschedule within that pattern. The final option is the end date for the recurrence. You can end after xx number of recurrences, by a certain date, or even have no end date.

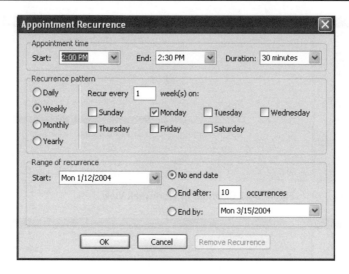

Figure 8-29 Appointment Recurrence Screen

The calendar is a great enhancement to your daily productivity. You can schedule your entire day. Although the default is for thirty minute time slots, the distance between time slots can be anywhere from five to sixty minutes. You can schedule an appointment at any specific time and for any specific length, regardless of the time slot you have selected.

For instance, you could schedule a racquetball game for every Thursday at 6:00 pm. The screen shots on the next page illustrate this procedure, which provides a good example of using recurrence in your appointments.

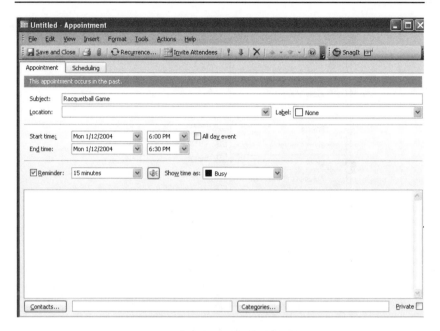

Figure 8-30 Recurring Appointments

Set the start time, end time, and reminder time. If you have chosen fifteen minutes as the default reminder time, that will be the first choice, but you can choose any reminder time from 0 minutes to two weeks.

You can set the time to show as free, tentative, busy, or out of office. The selected time frame is indicated by shading.

Figure 8-31 Show Time As Options

Label Colors

Calendar items can also be color-coded. This makes spotting particular items an easy chore. The different colors are shown on the following page along with what they stand for.

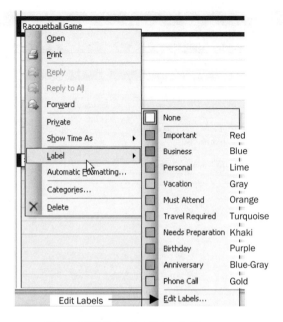

Figure 8-32 Calendar Color Options

The bottom selection in the preceding Figure is Edit Labels. By clicking this selection, you can redefine each of the labels to say something that is more personal and meaningful to you.

Contacts Folder

Is the Rolodex® on your desk overflowing with ragged index cards? Have some been lost because they no longer stay in the box? There is no longer a need to worry about them. Outlook can solve all of your Rolodex® headaches.

Adding a Contact

With all Outlook applications, you create a new item by clicking on New New ▾ (generally in the upper left corner). That's how you create a new contact, too.

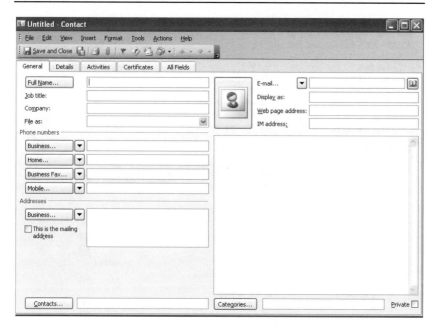

Figure 8-33 Creating a New Contact

Now pull out one of those ragged cards and start putting the information in a new contact. Is it a little hard to fit three addresses and 19 telephone numbers on that card? Not in Outlook. The amount of information available for a contact is basically as unlimited as a person's creativity.

The Details tab (which we'll go into more "detail" about later) lets you add additional information that you may have gathered on a contact.

Now that you have entered the information on your Rolodex card in a new contact, let's go over another method of creating a contact. Suppose you have e-mails from twenty of those Rolodex® contacts in the Inbox. Creating a contact from an e-mail is as simple as dragging the e-mail over to the Contacts section of the Navigation Pane!

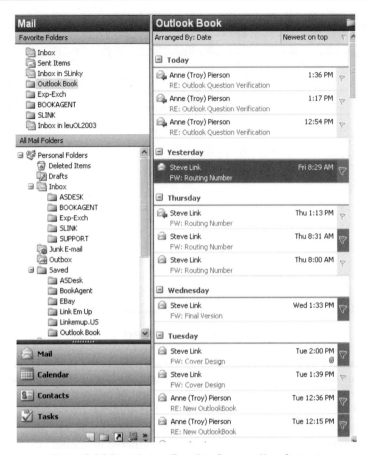

Figure 8-34 Dragging an E-mail to Create a New Contact

Tip: You can drag a highlighted message from the Inbox pane to the Contacts bar in the left pane. Outlook creates a new contact for you with as much information filled in as possible. For instance, it automatically populates the name and e-mail address for you.

Viewing Contacts

Your contacts list(s) could contain only the e-mail addresses to which you send messages.

Figure 8-35 Contact List in Address Cards View

The contents could also consist of your entire Rolodex© complete with addresses, phone numbers, notes, job title, company, and all the rest. That view is pictured below.

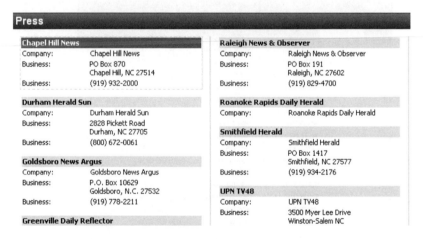

Figure 8-36 Contact List in Detailed Address Cards View

The Current View that you select determines which view you see. The view just above is called Detailed Address Cards while the first one shown is entitled simply Address Cards. Phone List is another quite useful view. It is pictured on the following page.

Press

			Full Name	Company	File As	Business Phone	Business Fax	Home Phone
				Click here t...				
				WITN Channel 7	WITN Channel 7			
				WCTI TV12	WCTI TV12	(252) 638-1212		
				WNCT TV9	WNCT TV9	(252) 355-8500		
				UPN TV48	UPN TV48	(336) 274-4848		
				WNCN TV17	WNCN TV17	(919) 836-1717		
				WRAZ TV50	WRAZ TV50	919) 595-5050		
				Wilson Daily Times	Wilson Daily Times	(252) 243-5151		
				Raleigh News & Ob...	Raleigh News & O...	(919) 829-4700		
				Chapel Hill News	Chapel Hill News	(919) 932-2000		
				Smithfield Herald	Smithfield Herald	(919) 934-2176		
				New Bern Sun Jour...	New Bern Sun Jou...	252) 638-8101		
				Kinston Free Press	Kinston Free Press	252) 527-3191		
				Greenville Daily Re...	Greenville Daily Re...			
				Goldsboro News Ar...	Goldsboro News A...	(919) 778-2211		
				Durham Herald Sun	Durham Herald Sun	(800) 672-0061		

Figure 8-37 Contact List in Phone List View

Address cards can be sorted by any of the columns. The same list is shown below sorted by business phone number.

Figure 8-38 Phone List View Sorted by Business Phone Number

Viewing Contact Records

Using the General Tab

The General Tab for a contact record shows about as much information as you could possibly imagine for a contact.

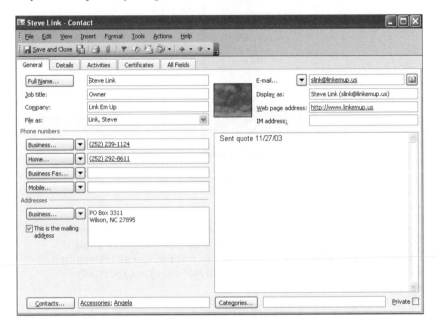

Figure 8-39 Contact Record, General Tab

Telephone List

By clicking on the down arrow button beside a phone number, you can choose from nineteen (yes, 19!) different telephone numbers for each contact (see the following Figure). Notice that each phone number that has been filled in has a check beside it. Although nineteen phone numbers are the default (and are probably more than you need), you can add even more through custom fields.

Figure 8-40 Phone List

Address List

Addresses function the same way. There are three different addresses that you can enter (see below). You choose which one displays using a drop-down selector. To choose which one you want to use as the mailing address, check the "This is the mailing address" checkbox (partially covered by the dropdown list.

Figure 8-41 Address List

Categories

You can assign a contact to different categories, as illustrated on the following page. Choose which categories a contact belongs to by checking the appropriate boxes. See the following Figure.

Figure 8-42 Categories Screen

Categories are completely user-definable. Clicking on the Master Category List button displays the complete list and allows you to modify the categories available. You can add more and delete the defaults until the only categories remaining are truly useful to you.

Figure 8-43 Master Category List

Contact Pictures

Outlook lets you add a picture of each contact so that you can visualize the person to whom you are talking. What is shown here is a nice sky picture. You could also use a company logo in place of an actual picture.

Tip: Use the area below the IM address to add notes. You can even drag documents associated with the contact into this area!

You can add notes and even drag documents associated with a contact to the notes area. ——▶ Sent quote 11/27/03

Figure 8-44 Excerpt from Contact Record, General Tab

Using the Details Tab

The Details tab shows still more information on the contact. For instance, if you use Outlook to manage sales contacts, you would want to know the spouse's name, birthday, and anniversary. Notice the Internet Free/Busy and Online NetMeeting settings. These can help to integrate the scheduling capabilities of Outlook for two coworkers separated by states (or even countries).

Figure 8-45 Contact Record, Details Tab

Using the Activities Tab

The Activities tab is also quite useful. It shows e-mail, appointments, tasks, journal, and notes associated with this contact. If you want to open an item in this window, just double-click on it. Regardless of which folder it is in, the item opens.

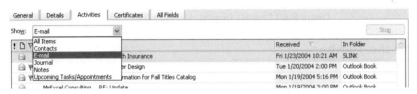

Figure 8-46 Contact Record, Activities Tab

Using the Certificates Tab

Here is the Certificates tab. A certificate is a digital ID that is attached to an e-mail. Each sender will have a different certificate, which guarantees that an individual e-mail is from that address, ensures that the e-mail has not been tampered with, and keeps it from being viewed by someone without the appropriate recipient certificate.

Figure 8-47 Contact Record, Certificates Tab

Using the All Fields Tab

The All Fields tab allows viewing of all of the fields in Outlook. These are grouped into user-defined Address fields, E-mail fields, and many others. Some fields belong to two or more groups. You can modify the fields in this view, also.

Figure 8-48 Contact Record, All Fields Tab

Using the Toolbar

The toolbar has quite a few interesting functions on it. The red flag you see here lets you flag a contact or e-mail with a specific color. You can define what the colors mean and what action is to be taken for items flagged in a certain way.

The yellow street sign you see beside the red flag allows you to look up an address on the web and map it. This would be quite useful if you need to visit a client and want driving directions.

Clicking the telephone dials the contact's phone number for you. With the proper equipment, you may never have to dial a number manually again!

Figure 8-49 Contact Record, Toolbar

You can associate contacts together using the Contacts button at the bottom of the screen. In this case, Accessories and the Angela contact are connected to this associate.

Figure 8-50 Contacts Button

Tools Menu Options

You can set up some contact options by clicking on Tools–Options and selecting the Preferences tab. The following Figure shows part of the screen shot you should see.

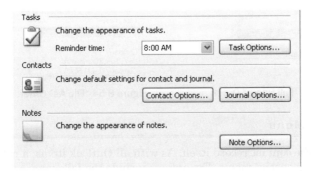

Figure 8-51 Excerpt from Tools, Options, Preferences Tab

Clicking on the Contact Options button displays the following choices.

Figure 8-52 Contact Options

The additional Contacts Index adds an additional language (font) for contacts.

You may want to display the contacts in a different order or change the default "File As" order. Those two options are shown on the following page.

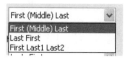

Figure 8-53 "Full Name" Order   **Figure 8-54 "File As" Order**

Right-click Menu

Now back to the contact record itself. As with all Outlook items, a right-click produces a special menu. The options include the following:

- Open (same as double-clicking)
- Print
- Forward
- New Message to Contact
- New Appointment with Contact
- New Meeting Request to Contact
- New Task for Contact
- New Journal Entry for Contact

- Link (link items to a contact)
- Items
- File
- Call Contact
- Call Using Netmeeting
- Follow Up
- Categories
- Delete

You can perform many of these selections using a button on the toolbar. The right-click menu gives you still more choices for getting things done.

> Tip: This sampling also shows how integrated the different functions of Office are. Basically, you can perform any function on an item from anywhere. Sending an e-mail to a contact you just called is only a right-click away...

Distribution Lists

Another method of grouping contacts together is called a Distribution List. In its most minimal sense, this is a list of contacts that share one or more common features. Two procedures for creating a Distribution List are covered below—manually and from an e-mail.

Creating a New Distribution List Manually

1. To create a new distribution list manually, click on the arrow beside New (usually in the upper left hand corner) and then click Distribution List.

Figure 8-55 New Menu

2. The screen that displays allows you to name the new list and to add its members.

Figure 8-56 Name a New Distribution List and Add Members

3. After naming the list (we will call it Outlook Book) and adding the members, click Save and Close.

Tip: When addressing a new e-mail, you can select this list by typing its name in one of the addressing fields (TO, CC, BCC). All recipients specified in the list will receive the e-mail.

Creating a distribution list from an e-mail

1. To create a distribution list from an existing e-mail, open an e-mail that has a list of contacts you want in a Distribution List. Highlight the names you to be added in the TO, CC, or BCC fields. Click Edit and then Copy (or the keyboard shortcut CTRL-C).

2. Now click on File, New, and select Distribution List. Name the list and click on Select Members.

3. Right-click on the Members box (at the bottom) to open a shortcut menu. Choose Paste (or CTRL-V as the keyboard shortcut).

New Contact from Same Company

Adding multiple contacts for one company is extremely easy with Outlook 2003. Under the Actions menu, you'll find the New Contact From Same Company option. This creates a new contact with the same company name, address, and phone numbers already filled in. Using this option, you don't have to enter all of that information again. You can, of course, change anything that differs.

Calling a Contact

Here is an option to automatically call a contact that you are viewing.

1. Under the Actions menu select Call Contact. A list of phone numbers displays for the contact on your screen.

2. Select one of those numbers. The screen below displays.

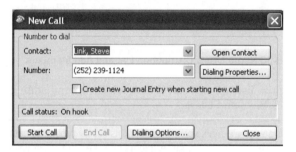

Figure 8-57 New Call Screen

3. From this screen you can view all contact information using the Open Contact button. Dialing Properties allows you to modify the properties of the modem connection. The Start Call button begins dialing and opens a new journal entry if that box is selected.

4. The Dialing Options button presents a screen for setting up speed dial entries. It is shown on the following page.

Figure 8-58 Dialing Options Screen

Notice that setting up speed dial entries in Outlook is much easier than programming them into a standard cordless, wireless, or wired phone. Dialing properties displays the area code properties while Line Properties allows modification of the modem setup.

Notice also that the Call status says On hook (see Figure 8-57). The modem is actually in use for the Internet connection in this instance, but Outlook does not know it. If Outlook had already initiated a call, the status would be Off hook.

> Tip: The Call Contact option works only if you have a modem in your computer that is properly configured and not already in use for some other function.

Creating a vCard from a Contact

It's easy to create a vCard from a contact. A vCard is like a virtual Rolodex card that you can send out via the Internet.

1. Open the contact for whom you want to create a vCard.

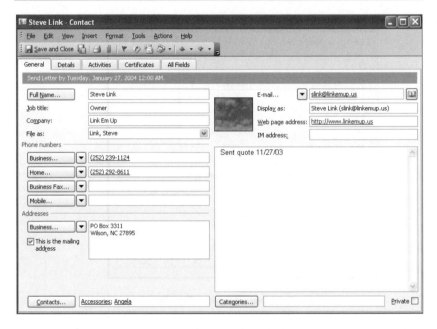

Figure 8-59 Contact Screen

2. Click on File-Export to vCard file.

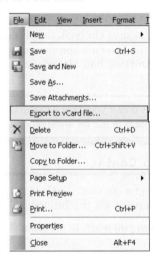

Figure 8-60 Export to vCard File

3. Name the file, and you have created a vCard for use in your e-mail signature(s) and elsewhere.

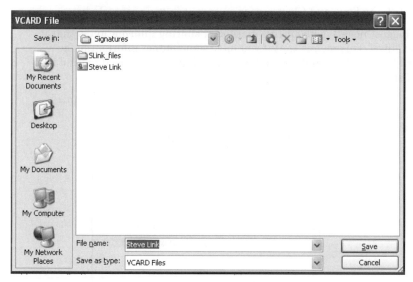

Figure 8-61 Creating a vCard

To illustrate another use for vCard let's set up a scenario. You are talking to a business associate who is asking about getting some signs printed up. You just received some new signs from a local business and are very impressed with the quality and customer service you received. You tell your associate and he asks for the name of the business, phone number, etc. All you need to say is "check your email." Send this contact record to him as a vCard and he can add it to his Contacts faster than you can say the name of the business (which, by the way is Wizzy Whatchit's Sign Services of America, LLP).

Forwarding as a vCard

The sharing of contacts is mentioned in another chapter of the book (see Sharing Calendars and Contacts on page 9-16.) You have various ways to accomplish this. One method of sharing contacts is Forward as vCard. If a contact is forwarded to you as a vCard, you receive it in a regular e-mail as an attachment.

1. Double-click on the attachment and verify that it is from a trusted source by choosing to Open it from the security prompt.

2. Click the Save and Close button to save it in your contacts list.

The biggest negative about this method of sharing information is that it is not "live." This means that if you have sent contact information as a vCard to five others and your information changes, you need to send it to all of them again.

If you receive a contact that is a duplicate of an already existing entry, Outlook shows you the screen below after you choose to Save and Close.

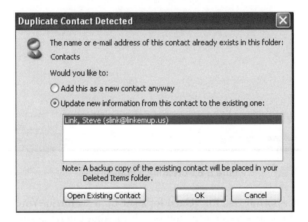

Figure 8-62 Duplicate Contact Detected Screen

Adding this item as a new contact could create massive confusion in the contacts list. That is the reason the Update option is the default selection. If you need to verify that the information is the same (before doing the update) you can choose the Open Existing Contact button.

Address Books

You can also view contacts through the Address Book. For this option, click on Tools and then Address Book. A screen similar to the following one displays.

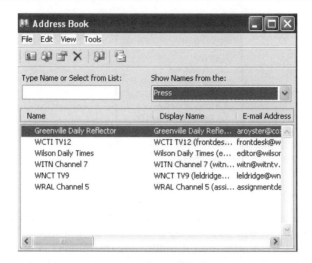

Figure 8-63 Address Book Showing Contacts

Notice that all listings shown have e-mail addresses. The main functionality for the address book is to facilitate e-mail.

Notice also that Press is selected in the "Show Names from the" box. This selector lists all of the different folders displayed under Contacts. You can select an address either by scrolling or by typing the desired name in the Type Name ... box.

Once you find the desired name, you can double-click on it to display the full contact record.

Deleted Items Folder

This is basically a "trash can", and it works the same way as the wastebasket you have at the end of your desk. Five thousand e-mails can be deleted and they will remain there until you empty the deleted items folder. The good thing about this feature is that you can say "oops, I didn't mean to delete that," and take it from deleted items back into your inbox. The bad thing is that many people hardly ever empty their deleted items. The following figure shows a Deleted Items box that appears quite normal.

Figure 8-64 Deleted Items Box

Notice that there are only two unread messages. Unread messages are marked by the folder's name appearing in bold (indicating unread items) and a number in parentheses after it (indicating the number of unread messages). It looks good until you see the whole list of items that are in there.

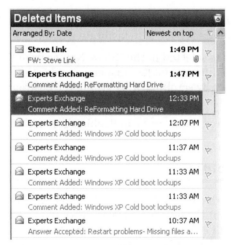

Figure 8-65 Deleted Items Screen

Above you see the two unread messages in bold, but there are actually 326 items in the deleted items folder. This folder can easily fill up and waste space and efficiency if you don't clean it out regularly.

Deleting Items

There are a few different ways for you to keep your deleted items cleaned up. One option is to tell Outlook to automatically empty deleted items when exiting (this is the easiest, most automatic method). Do this by selecting Tools–Options and then clicking on the Other tab. A portion of it is pictured below.

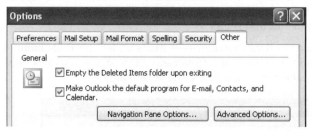

Figure 8-66 Options Screen

You can also delete items manually by using the Empty Deleted Items option in the Tools menu to clean up the deleted items.

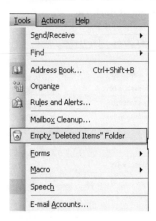

Figure 8-67 Tools Menu, Empty "Deleted Items" Folder

The third option for cleaning up your deleted items and mailbox in general is to use the Mailbox Cleanup Wizard. Clicking the Empty button in the Mailbox Cleanup wizard empties your deleted Items folder. You can also view the size of the deleted items before you delete them. The wizard is discussed in greater detail under Special Features, Using the Mailbox Cleanup Wizard on page 9-28.

Drafts Folder

The Drafts folder is where Outlook stores any unfinished e-mails. The default for Outlook 2003 is to automatically store any e-mails that are exited before being sent in the Drafts folder. That way you can recall them later, then edit and send.

You can change the behavior of unsent items under the Tools menu. Click on Options and then choose the Preferences tab. When you click on the E-mail Options button, you will see the screen below.

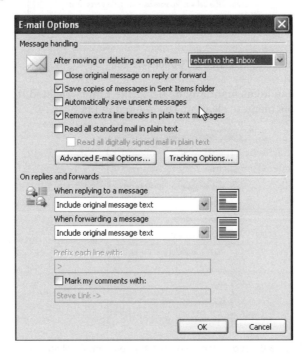

Figure 8-68 Options, Preferences, E-mail Options Screen

Notice that Automatically save unsent messages is unchecked. With this setting, Outlook prompts you whenever you close out an unsent message.

Figure 8-69 Save Unsent Message Prompt

You can set more save options by clicking on the Advanced E-mail Options button. The following screen displays.

Figure 8-70 Excerpt from Advanced E-mails Options Screen

You can specify a different location for saving unsent items and change the Autosave feature as well as other settings.

Inbox Folder

The Inbox is where all of your e-mail is received.

Delivery Options

You can select a new mail delivery location other than the Inbox through the Tools–E-Mail Accounts menu selection. It displays a screen with a View or Change selection. Select that, and then click Next. You will see the following screen.

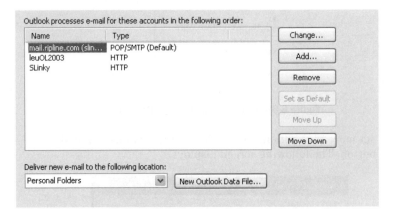

Figure 8-71 View or Change Selection Screen

Near the bottom of the screen is a Deliver new e-mail to the following location option. It is set to Personal Folders here but could be changed to an Exchange Server account, archive folders, etc.

Right-click E-mail Menu Options

Right-clicking on an e-mail item produces the following options:

- Open
- Print
- Reply
- Reply to All
- Forward
- Follow-Up
- Red Flag
- Blue Flag

- Yellow Flag
- Green Flag

- Orange Flag

- Purple Flag
- Flag Complete

- Mark as Unread
- Categories
- Find All
- Related Messages
- Messages from Sender
- Create Rule
- Junk E-mail
- Add Sender to Blocked Senders List
- Add Sender to Safe Senders List
- Add Sender's Domain to Safe Senders List (@example.com)
- Add Recipient to Safe Recipients List
- Mark as Not Junk
- Junk E-mail Options

➤ Add Reminder
➤ Clear Flag
➤ Set Default Flag (the different colored flags are here also)

➤ Delete
➤ Move to Folder
➤ Options ...

The follow up flags are completely user-definable. One user may want to call a red flag item the most important, while another may reserve that status for the green flag. This is all based on the user's desires.

The Junk E-mail Options, Rule option makes it so easy to handle incoming e-mail. If something comes in that you consider junk e-mail, right-click and add the sender to blocked senders list. If everything from that domain is considered junk, add the domain instead of only the sender.

Another option that simplifies e-mail management tremendously is to create Rules. Placing this option on the right-click menu makes it readily available for e-mail-by-e-mail usage. Clicking on it produces a rules screen with all of the information already filled in.

Figure 8-72 Create Rule Screen

Creating a Rule is as simple as right-clicking and then selecting a few check boxes.

The move, copy, rename, and delete options are also in the right-click e-mail menu. Let's say that you want to move the entire structure and all messages to another folder. You can do this with one click on Move from the highest level to be moved.

Deleting the entire structure is just as easy. Right-click on the top level to be removed and verify that you want to delete that folder, all below it and all messages in all folders. Voila, they are all gone.

Using Search Folders

There are three folders that are new to Outlook 2003: Unread Mail, For Follow Up, and Large Mail folders. These are known as Search folders, which means that they don't actually contain the messages; they just contain links to them. If you delete one of these folders, the messages still exist in their original folder(s).

The default Search folders are:

➤ For Follow Up

➤ Large Mail

➤ Unread Mail

The For Follow Up folder contains a link to all e-mail flagged for follow up (with a Red, Blue, Yellow, Green, Orange, or Purple Flag) in all of the folders in the current mailbox. These messages are arranged by flag color.

The Large Mail folder also spans across all folders and contains a link to any e-mail that has a total size equal to or greater than 100 kilobytes. Generally this would indicate a moderately sized attachment. This could come in handy if the system is tight on disk space and larger e-mail needs to be easily disposed of.

The Unread Mail folder contains a link to all unread mail in all folders. In the instances where there are many folders and they all get a lot of activity, this could function as a real time saver. You may have fifty unread mail messages across ten different folders. Instead of having to browse through all ten folders, you can access the messages through the Unread Mail folder.

You can also create custom Search folders. In this section, we will create a custom Search folder for important mail received from sclaus@linkemup.us with one or more attachments.

1. Right-click on the Search Folders folder under All Mail Folders and then choose New Search Folder. You'll see the screen below.

Figure 8-73 New Search Folder Screen

2. Click on Create a custom Search folder (shown highlighted) and then click on Choose to start the process.

3. We will name this folder Important SClaus. Click Criteria to select which e-mails this will show.

4. In the From field, type sclaus@linkemup.us and then click on the More Choices tab.

5. Check Only items with: and select One or more attachments.

6. Check Whose Importance is: and select High.

7. Click on OK three times.

Now we have created a custom Search folder. Of course, you should create something applicable to your e-mail habits.

When creating a Search folder, some of the options to choose from include Mail with attachments, Mail from specific people, and Mail received this week. A Search folder is a saved search that is kept up-to-date, spanning across all folders and pointing to the items that match the search criteria.

You can also create a Search folder by starting with a search using Find.

1. Click on Tools, Find, and Find again to open the Find bar.

2. Create a search criterion and execute it by clicking Find Now.

3. After execution, click on Options and select Save As Search Folder (as shown below).

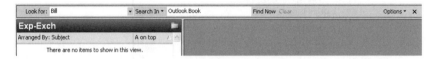

Figure 8-74 Search Folder

4. Next name the folder and click OK. This folder will now show up in the Search Folders listing.

All Search folders can be customized. Right click on the Search Folder to change and then left click on Customize This Search Folder. A screen like the one displayed below appears.

Figure 8-75 Custom Search Folder

You can change the folders included in the search by clicking the Browse button. Multiple folders can be included along with searching all sub-folders.

Journal Folder

The Journal is really quite a useful tool in the Outlook program. Using the journal, you can track tasks, documents, phone calls, and many other things associated with a contact.

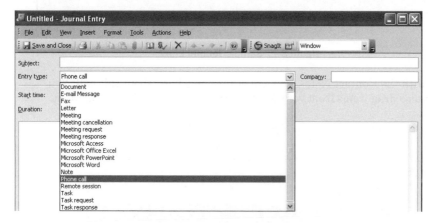

Figure 8-76 Journal Entry Types

A journal entry somewhat duplicates the functionality of the Activities tab in Contacts. It is actually complementary to Activities because it allows each item to be viewed in a chronological order. See below for a sample journal entry for a phone call to discuss Outlook (as indicated by the subject and entry type).

This phone call is being timed. Notice that the timer has been started (by clicking on the timer icon to the right of the Start Timer/Pause Timer buttons). The duration automatically increments as each minute passes by.

Figure 8-77 Sample Journal Entry

As with the Contact Notes, you can enter notes here about this call. You can also drag items from your My Documents folder to the journal item.

Figure 8-78 Adding Notes and Documents to a Journal Item

You should exercise caution when you are storing documents with journal items, contacts, or other entries. The size of your mailbox file increases with each item that you add. Notice that the file I added here is only 6k in size (the number in parentheses beside of it). The size of the mailbox file on my hard drive was also increased by that same amount.

Click on the Contacts button to select the appropriate contact for this call.

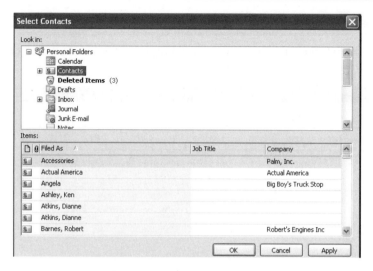

Figure 8-79 Selecting a Contact

Click on the Categories button to assign a category to this call.

Figure 8-80 Selecting Categories

Viewing Journal Entries

As with other Outlook items, you can view Journal entries in a number of formats. One optional view of your data is daily.

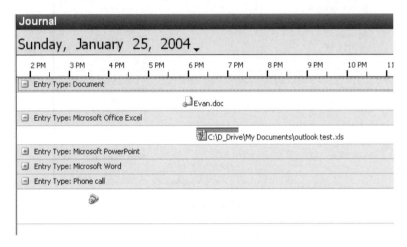

Figure 8-81 Journal Entry in Daily View

Right-clicking on the date area allows you to choose a different view along with filter, sort, and other options.

Figure 8-82 Journal Entry Right-click Options

Below you see the same journal entries in a weekly view ...

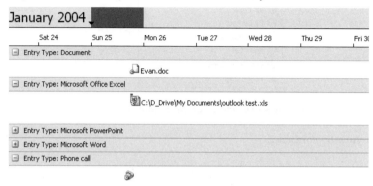

Figure 8-83 Journal Entry in Weekly View

... and a monthly view.

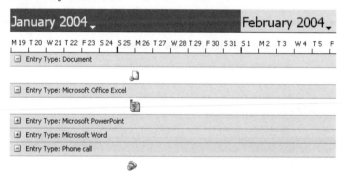

Figure 8-84 Journal Entry in Monthly View

The Journal views shown so far have been by type. The following Figures show you the same information in a weekly view by contact and by category.

Figure 8-85 Selecting Current Journal View

Here is a view by contact ...

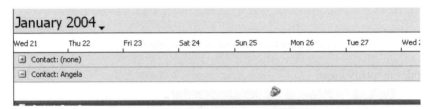

Figure 8-86 Journal View by Contact

... and by category.

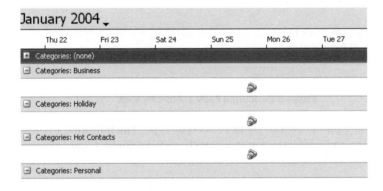

Figure 8-87 Journal View by Category

You can set up journal options by clicking on the Tools menu option. Now click on Options and select the Preferences tab. The following is a partial view of the screen shot that displays.

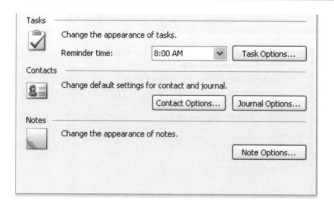

Figure 8-88 Setting Journal Options

Clicking on the Journal Options button displays the following screen.

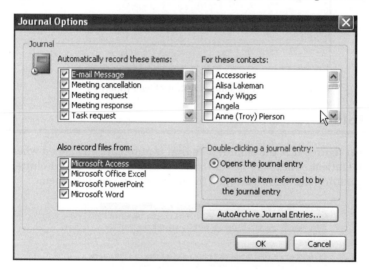

Figure 8-89 Journal Options Screen

The Journal Options screen lets you choose which items to automatically record in the journal as well as the contacts for which you want to track journal entries. The AutoArchive Journal Entries button displays the Journal Properties screen. This screen provides you with the ability to decide when and where to archive items out of the journal.

Figure 8-90 Setting Journal AutoArchive Properties

Notes Folder

See the next figure? It is the default note that is automatically added when you install Outlook. These are better than "sticky notes" – you don't clutter up your monitor with them. You open them only when you need them.

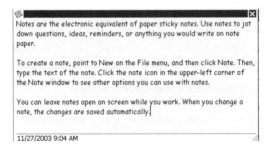

Figure 8-91 Default Note

The Notes folder view is pictured on the following page.

Figure 8-92 Notes Folder View

This view displays all of the notes you have entered. You can open a note by double-clicking on it. In most cases only a portion of the note will be displayed in a small area. You can enlarge a note by putting your mouse cursor over the lower right corner (with the ◿ symbol), left-clicking and dragging. The note itself can be resized in all four directions. The text within the note expands or compresses with the size of the box.

Figure 8-93 Initial Note Display

Notice that the note in the smaller version above looks like it is the complete note. There is no scroll bar or anything else to indicate that there may be more text. You will only know that there is more to the note by dragging the resize bar. Below you see the entire note in a single screen.

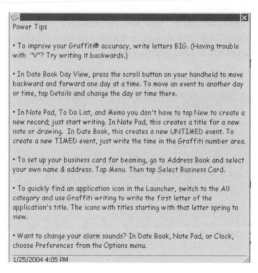

Figure 8-94 Enlarged Note display

Left-click Options

Left-clicking on a note in the upper left corner allows you to change many of the properties of an individual note.

Figure 8-95 Note Left-click Options

In the previous note screen shots, the color was changed to pink. You can customize the color as you see fit.

You can assign categories and contacts to a note in the same manner as you would to journal entries. Also, like journal entries, you can view notes in different views. The Notes folder view you saw displayed previously was the Icon view (see Figure 8-92).

Figure 8-96 Selecting Current View for Notes

Here you see notes in list view ...

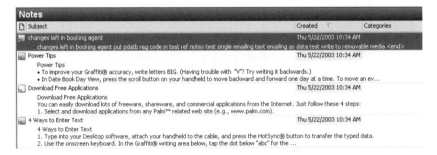

Figure 8-97 Notes in List View

... and here, viewed by color

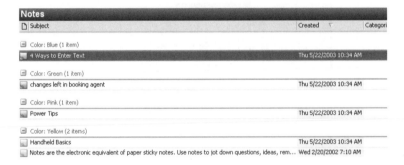

Figure 8-98 Notes in Color View

You can also set up options for notes by clicking on the Tools menu option, then clicking on Options and selecting the Preferences tab. See the next page for a partial shot of the screen that displays.

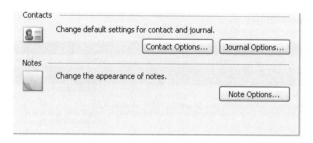

Figure 8-99 Setting Note Options

Clicking the Note Options button displays the screen below.

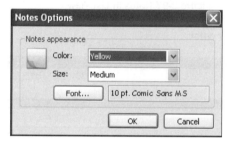

Figure 8-100 Note Options Screen

Outbox Folder

The Outbox is similar to your postal mailbox. You write a letter, address it, and place it in the mailbox, where it stays until the mail delivery person comes by to pick it up.

The Outbox is where Outlook stores your messages until it sends them.

Figure 8-101 Mail Favorite Folders

Mail Options

You can reach quite a few options to control sending and receiving mail from Tools–Options–Mail Setup tab. See below.

Figure 8-102 Options, Mail Setup Tab

If you uncheck Send immediately when connected, e-mail stays in the Outbox until you click the Send/Receive button ⟨Send/Receive ▾⟩ in the toolbar. Clicking on that button on the Mail Setup screen displays the following options.

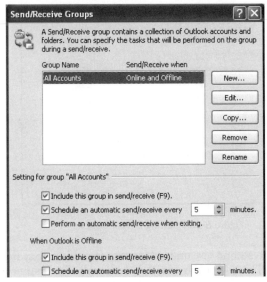

Figure 8-103 Setting Send/Receive Groups

This is the location for setting how often an automatic send/receive will occur. You also set the behavior of sending and receiving while offline in this screen.

Sent Items Folder

The Sent Items folder is a repository of the e-mails you have sent. If you're not careful, it could actually have all of the e-mails you have ever sent in it! It is important for you to properly maintain the Sent Items folder so that your disk space is not wasted.

Another option is to turn off the saving of sent e-mails. You can access this option through Tools–Options–E-mail Options. The following screen displays.

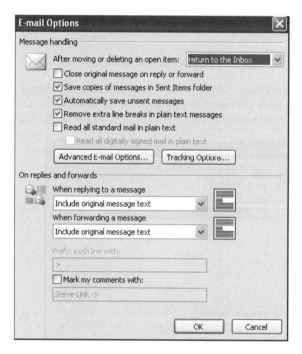

Figure 8-104 Setting E-mail Options

If you un-check the second box under Message Handling, sent messages will not be saved. This is not recommended, though. For instance, you may have an important e-mail that was forwarded to your boss. The only

way to verify that it was not modified before it reached him/her is to view
what you originally sent from Sent Items folder.

Within the Sent Items Properties, there are quite a few options. Right
click on Sent Items and left-click on Properties to see the Sent Item
Properties screen.

Figure 8-105 Sent Item Properties

If you select the Show total number of items option, a number displays
beside Sent Items that indicates the number of items in the folder;
otherwise, a number shows only if there are unread items.

The Folder Size button displays the size of all the items in this folder.
The Sent Items folder could use hundreds of megabytes if it is not
maintained properly.

The AutoArchive functionality is extremely important for this folder. One
of the best settings is to autoarchive the Sent Items every three weeks
and to send them to Deleted Items. Using this method, after three weeks
you no longer have to worry about them since they are automatically
deleted.

Resend This Message

A handy option (located in the Actions menu) to use for Sent Items is Resend This Message. Opening a message in the Sent Items folder and then selecting this option from the Actions menu opens the message just as if it were created as a new message. The recipient(s) will already be filled in along with anything else that was populated in the original message.

This works well if the Internet connection failed when you were sending the message and you need to resend it. Another function of this feature allows you to send a message on a weekly basis. You can even send the same message to different people (based on sales figures, perhaps). Using Resend This Message and changing the recipient(s) lets you accomplish this task with ease.

You can also choose Resend This Message on messages that are in folders other than Sent Items. If you do this on a message where you are not the original sender, Outlook displays a "safety prompt" asking if you want to resend it anyway. If you resend the message, the message appears as "xxx on behalf of yyy."

Recall This Message

When looking in the Sent Items folder, you may come across an e-mail and say "OOPS! I didn't mean to send that."

You can attempt to recall the message by opening it and clicking on the Actions menu and Recall This Message. The screen shown below pops up.

Figure 8-106 Recalling a Message

As noted, if the recipient has already read the message, there is nothing that can be done. To complete the recall, the recipient has to acknowledge and approve the recall. If the recipient is nosy (as most probably are), the recall will fail because they will have read the message before the recall notice arrived or they will cancel the recall.

Recall sometimes works if there is an Exchange Server between the sender and recipient and the message hasn't been read. In testing this process through the Internet, all my attempts at message recall failed. Outlook returned the following message (because I checked the checkbox above):

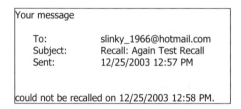

Your message	
To:	slinky_1966@hotmail.com
Subject:	Recall: Again Test Recall
Sent:	12/25/2003 12:57 PM

could not be recalled on 12/25/2003 12:58 PM.

Figure 8-107 Recall Failed Message

Tasks Folder

Tasks can be used for basically the same purposes as Calendar. The biggest difference is that you don't assign an expected duration for the item. However, you still set Start Date, Due Date, Reminder Start Time, Recurrence, and other selections.

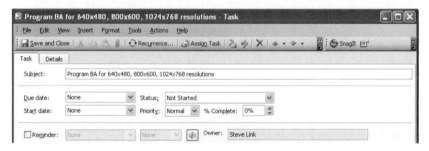

Figure 8-108 Task Screen

Viewing Tasks

After setting up your tasks, you can view them in different formats. The list is pictured below. The Simple List, Detailed List, and Active Tasks views are pictured below in that order.

Figure 8-109 Tasks, Current View List

Figure 8-110 Tasks, Simple List View

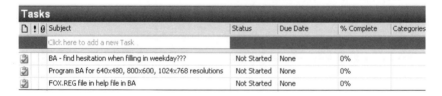

Figure 8-111 Tasks, Detailed List View

Notice that you have a percent complete, due date, and status pictured in the Active Tasks view. You can also view only active tasks, which screens out those that have been completed. The middle task pictured above has now been tagged as completed, so only two items show in the following Active Tasks view. There are two data views presented here – one with all three tasks showing, and the other with only two showing (see the screen shot on the next page) because one has been completed.

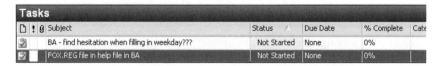

Figure 8-112 Tasks, Active Tasks View

Tasks works quite well for managing things that have to be done, but that don't have a real time frame for accomplishment. You may decide to put "Wash car ..." or "Take wife out to eat ..." in as a task. Either of these could take thirty minutes or two hours, depending on how much time you want to dedicate to them.

If you utilize a PDA, it should synchronize quite easily with Outlook on the desktop and allow you to carry all contacts, tasks, and calendar items with you everywhere you go.

Another excellent function with tasks is the ability to assign tasks to a particular person. This works well in an office environment that uses an Exchange Server to manage the Outlook data. If a task is assigned to someone, they will receive it as an e-mail. The procedure below illustrates that process.

1. With Tasks selected, click on Actions and then New Task Request.

2. Fill this out and click Send. The task is added to the sender's task list and an E-mail that looks similar to the shot below will arrive in the recipient's inbox.

Figure 8-113 Task Sent as E-mail

Notice the Accept and Decline buttons at the top. Once a recipient accepts the task, it is added to his or her task list. The recipient can occasionally send a status for this task by clicking on Actions and Send Status Report (using the percent completed field to indicate the status).

Task Recurrence

The recurrence settings for a task are almost the same as those for a calendar item. The difference is that tasks have to be regenerated after being completed. Notice that the tasks are reassigned with a due date one week after completion.

The recurrence screen for a task is shown on the following page.

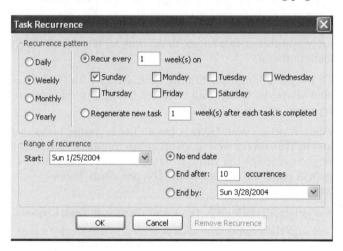

Figure 8-114 Task Recurrence Screen

The reason for this is so that the setting will recur every week on Sunday. If the Regenerate new task option is selected, the new task will not be regenerated until the designated number of weeks (in this case, one) after the date it was tagged as complete.

Figure 8-115 Tasks, Recurrent Tasks

Turning An E-mail Into a Task

If a coworker sends an e-mail and invites you to a Christmas party, there are two locations this invitation can be placed – in a task or on the calendar. In this section we will create a task from an e-mail.

1. Drag the message from the Inbox to the Tasks item on the left side. A new task opens with the message as the body.
2. Choose the due date for this event.
3. Click on Save and Close and the new task is created.

This page intentionally left blank.

9. Special Features

Designing Forms and Templates

Changing Contact Forms

With a Contact item open, you can modify the form you are using to view and edit that item. Click on the Tools menu item and then Forms–Design This Form.

A screen displays, similar to the one shown below.

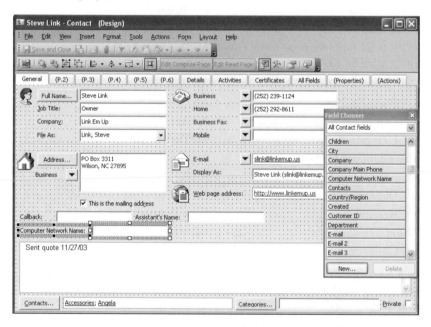

Figure 9-1 Changing Contact Forms

In this example, the Notes field has been shortened and the IM Address field has been deleted. Assistant's Name, Callback, and Computer Network Name have been added using the Field Chooser. There are different groupings of fields within the Field Chooser.

You choose these groupings using the drop-down box. They are listed below (with samples below some groupings).

- Frequently Used fields
  - Business address
  - Company
  - Full Name
  - Address fields
  - Home Address
  - Mailing Address
  - Street Address
- E-mail fields
  - E-mail
  - E-mail Address Type
  - E-mail Display As
- Fax/Other Number fields
  - Business Fax
  - Computer Network Name
  - FTP Site
- Miscellaneous fields
  - Assistant's Name
  - Department
  - Reminder
- Name fields
  - Children

- Job Title
- Nickname
- Personal fields
  - Anniversary
  - Hobbies
  - Referred By
- Phone Number fields
  - Car Phone
  - Pager
  - Primary Phone
- All Document fields
- All Mail fields
- All Post fields
- All Contact fields
- All Appointment fields
- All Task fields
- All Journal fields
- All Note fields
- All Distribution List fields
- User Defined fields in folder
- Forms

These fields can be repeated in multiple groupings. There are no example fields listed in the All ... fields because they contain all the fields that are associated with that particular group.

Notice the User Defined fields in folder group. If you need a field that is not listed by default, you can create it, then show and use it on the form. Maybe your company needs an Expires Date for its subscription service. The procedure below will create that date field and place it on the form for you.

1. Select User Defined fields in folder and click on New.

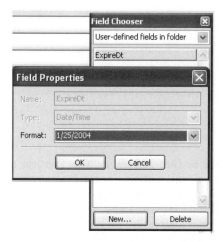

Figure 9-2 Creating a New User-defined Field

2. Name the field ExpireDt, set the Type to Date/Time type and the Format as shown above. Click OK.

3. Now drag that field onto the form and place it in the proper location.

4. On the menu, click Tools–Forms–Publish Form As and put in a name. I don't recommend that you overwrite the default because the original may be needed later. Name it Contact2 and click Publish.

The next time you view this contact, it will display in the new form.

Creating E-mail Templates

Do you send the same message (possibly to the same people) on a regular basis? If so, you can really simplify this task by creating an e-mail template. In this section we will create a template for sending digital pictures to relatives. First, we need to verify that Word is not being used as the editor (creating an e-mail template does not seem to work well with Word as the editor). Click Tools–Options and then the Mail Format tab. Uncheck the Use Microsoft Office Word box and click OK.

1. Start by creating the usual new e-mail. Click the arrow beside New and choose E-mail from the drop down box and fill in any information that is going to be constant. In this case, To, Subject, and Body will be automatically filled in (as shown on the following page).

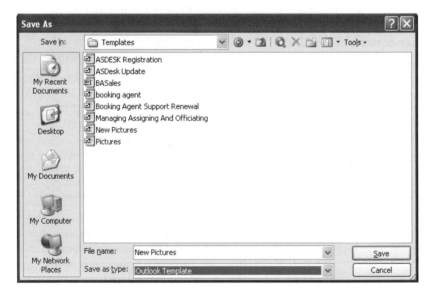

Figure 9-3 E-mail Template

This information will be sent with every New Pictures message. If you need to keep the e-mail addresses confidential, you can place them in the BCC field and put your own e-mail address in the To... field. BCC means Blind Courtesy Copy. You can use it to include recipients whose e-mail addresses will not be exposed to the others receiving the e-mail. This is handy because many people do not want their e-mail addresses given out. To respect their wishes, always put their e-mail addresses in the BCC field.

2. Click on File and Save As. Now select Outlook Template in the Save As Type box. Name the template and click on Save. Now that you have created a template, you can use it for new messages.

Figure 9-4 Saving a User-defined E-mail Template

3. Click on File, New, and Choose Form. After choosing User Templates in File System you will see a screen similar to the following.

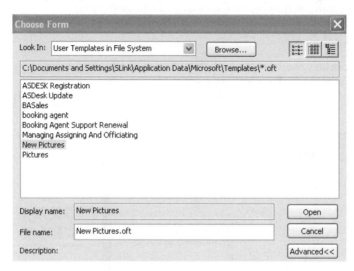

Figure 9-5 Choose Form Screen

4. As you can see from this screen, you can set many different e-mail templates for a variety of purposes. Click on New Pictures (or whatever name you assigned the new template) and then click Open.

5. A new message opens with the saved information already filled in. Since the purpose of this template is to send digital pictures, the only task left is attaching those pictures and clicking Send.

6. Now you may want to set the editor back to Word. Click Tools, Options, and the Mail Format tab. Check the Use Microsoft Office Word box and click OK.

Mapping an Address

Let's set up a scenario. You haven't talked to one of your business contacts in a while, so you decide to call him. The first thing to do (of course) is to pull up his record in Contacts so you can make the call. You chat for a while, wish him a happy anniversary (you also have this date in his contact record) and decide that you want to take him out to lunch the next week to discuss a new business proposal.

You want this guy to believe you are knowledgeable about just about everything, so you don't bother to ask how to get to his office building. He works in a small town in North Carolina and the address is:

> 1911 Highway 117 South
> Goldsboro, NC

While the contact record is open, click on Actions and then Display map of address or click 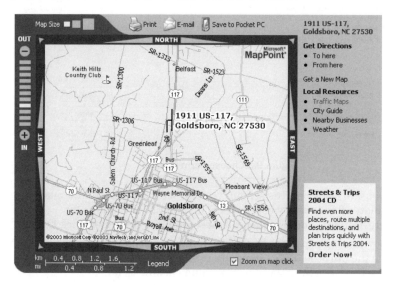. Your web browser opens, goes to http://mappoint.msn.com, and looks up the address for you. The map that displays will look something like the screen shot below.

Figure 9-6 Map to Contact Address

A nice feature of this (and most) mapping program(s) is the availability of driving directions. By clicking on the To here link under Get Directions (on the right) you can call up driving directions from here to anywhere. Of course, this most likely will not reflect construction detours and other temporary road modifications.

Flag For Follow Up

Let's set up another scenario. You have just finished an important discussion with a potential client. He closes with "Give me a week to think about it ..."

Do you write a note on your trusty legal pad to call back in a week (and lose it under a pile of other stuff)? No; instead, just click the Actions menu item and then Follow Up. A screen similar to the following one displays.

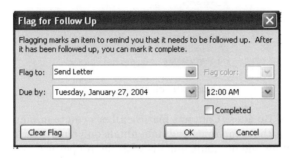

Figure 9-7 Flag for Follow Up

Another phone call could be considered "pushing it" but a follow-up letter would be nice. Choose the date and time to perform this action and click OK.

This displays the Follow Up flag in the contacts view.

Figure 9-8 Follow Up Flag

It also displays Send Letter by January 27, 2004 at 12:00 a.m. in the header area of the full-page view for that contact.

Business Contact Manager

Business Contact Manager comes bundled with the Office Small Business 2003 and Office Professional 2003 editions. It adds Contact Relationship Management (CRM) capabilities into Outlook and works well for businesses with twenty-five or fewer employees. This section gives an overview of the functionality gained from using Business Contact Manager.

Figure 9-9 Folder List

The Accounts and Business Contacts feature allows you to manage information about the companies and individuals on your client list. It associates incoming and outgoing e-mails with the proper account, contact, or opportunity for easy viewing of the history you have with that client. You can link appointments, tasks, notes, phone logs, and files to an account, contact, or opportunity. You can also reduce clutter and the chance of lost papers by scanning documents and associating them with a contact.

This feature lets you track sales more easily. It makes information such as sales stage, revenue potential, and probability of closing readily available to help maximize your sales. Customizable reports show you where an opportunity fits in the sales process, which helps you to prioritize your work. You can view only the most relevant information on your contacts and sales opportunities.

Reports filter and summarize information about contacts and opportunities. For example, a report can list the contacts you have not communicated with recently or provide the sales forecast for the next quarter. There are many built-in reports. If the exact information desired is not built into a report, you can create a customized report.

Installing Business Contact Manager

If your edition of Outlook includes Business Contact Manager (BCM), use the following steps to install it on your system.

1. Close Outlook.
2. Run Outlook with Business Contact Manager Setup and allow it to set up the .NET framework if asked.
3. If necessary, reboot to continue.
4. The BCM Installer will now run.

5. Run Outlook.

6. When prompted to associate BCM with your user account, click Yes. This is required to be able to use BCM.

Mail Merging with Word

Merging to a list of contacts is a quite simple task. You can merge form letters, mailing labels, envelopes, or a catalog and you can merge them to a new document, printer, or e-mail. First, you need to select the Tools menu and click on Mail Merge.

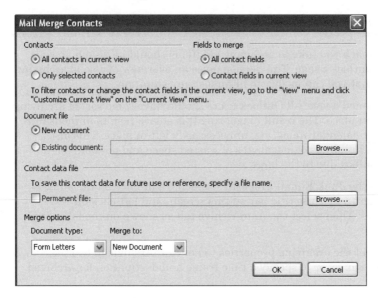

Figure 9-10 Mail Merge Contacts

This is the screen that is used to set up the merge. You can select the entire list or only certain contacts within the list. Also, you can select all fields, or you can choose only certain fields.

You make these selections by modifying the current data view. The procedure for defining data views is explained above Document File in the screen shot above and detailed in another chapter (see View Menu on page 4-4 and Customizing Views on page 5-30.

This feature uses a Microsoft Word document to actually perform the merge. Inserting merge fields and creating a form letter is quite simple and is explained in the Automation section of this book (see Creating E-mail Merges on page 11-3).

E-mail is another merge destination, as illustrated below.

Figure 9-11 Merge Options

Archiving Strategies

The approach you take to archiving old items should be unique to your specific Outlook usage. This section gives an overview of a solid archiving method that you can modify to fit almost any situation.

As mentioned above, all Outlook users should have some sort of archiving strategy in place. The result of ignoring this advice results in thousands of e-mails, calendar items, etc. unnecessarily left in place. This also results in hundreds of megabytes of wasted space and possible corruption of the mailbox due to the large size.

To get to the Junk E-mail Properties screen, right-click on the Junk E-mail folder (notice the title bar on this screen) and left-click on Properties. Then select the AutoArchive tab as shown on the following page.

You can set the archiving properties to not AutoArchive, to use the default settings, or to specify a time frame and destination for archived items.

This screen shows a selection that archives items older than three days and permanently deletes them. This setting is not suitable for a normal, functional folder; but it is fine for the Junk E-mail folder because that generally contains only unsolicited e-mail.

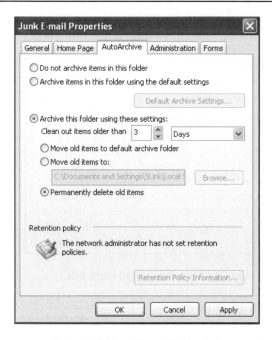

Figure 9-12 Junk E-mail Properties

The suggested setting for a "normal" folder would be to archive every three months and to move the items to the default archive folder. This way old items are moved out of the normally viewed area but are still available if you want to review them again.

The Mailbox Cleanup Wizard, accessed under the Tools menu, also offers archiving capabilities. Clicking the AutoArchive button in the Mailbox Cleanup screen forces the current archive rules to run at that time.

An additional Mailbox Cleanup option is View Deleted Items size. You may notice that the Folder Size screen shown on the next page gives you the same information that you see in the Mailbox Size option. The difference here is that View Deleted Items only displays the deleted items and folders beneath that folder, if there are any.

You also have the ability to empty deleted items from the Mailbox Cleanup screen. If you click on the Empty button, your deleted items are gone, never to be seen again.

For additional information on the Mailbox Cleanup, see Using the Mailbox Cleanup Wizard on page 9-28.

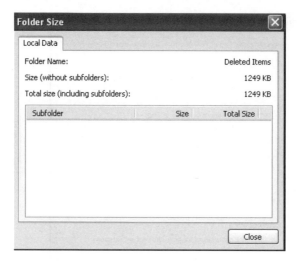

Figure 9-13 Viewing Deleted Items Size

Performing Send/Receive

There may be five different accounts set up in Outlook, but only two can be checked automatically. The others are checked only at certain times. You can perform a send/receive For Only One Account on these other accounts in two ways.

The first way uses an individual Send/Receive, which you can access through the Tools menu. Below is a screen shot of the various Send/Receive options.

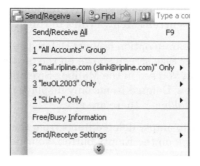

Figure 9-14 Send/Receive Options

Clicking on Send/Receive All (or pressing F9) checks all the e-mail accounts. Clicking on an individual installed account allows a Send and/or Receive for that account only.

In order to set up checking for only certain accounts using this method, you first need to disable automatic checking. This is an option under the Send/Receive Settings option.

The second alternative for activating only certain accounts is to set up groups. You can access the screenshot below (Send/Receive Settings – Test) by clicking on Define Send/Receive Groups under the Send/Receive Settings option. That action displays the Send/Receive Groups screen.

Click on the New button to create a new group. In this instance, we will create a Test group.

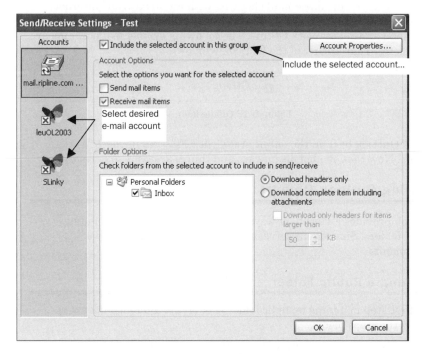

Figure 9-15 Send/Receive Settings Screen

Select the desired e-mail account in the left section and check the Include the selected account... box to enable the options on the right side.

Notice that this account will only receive mail items and will download headers only. To speed the download process, you can use the download headers only option for large e-mails. This option provides an Internet Message Access Protocol (IMAP) sort of functionality. IMAP is a mail service where all of the e-mail is kept on the server. It is similar to HTTP mail (such as Hotmail) in that respect as well as the fact that it assists in making e-mail access portable.

By setting up this group, you can schedule Outlook to automatically check only these accounts and to ignore the others.

There may be times when you want to disable e-mail checking completely. If the Internet connection is dial-up, you can easily accomplish this by disconnecting.

But how can you disable e-mail checking with an "always on" Internet connection such as DSL or cable? Quite easily, once again. Click on the File menu and select Work Offline. The following symbol will now appear in the lower right corner of the Outlook window.

Figure 9-16 Offline Icon

To put Outlook back in the online state, click File and uncheck Work Offline. Now that symbol disappears and things are back to normal.

Sharing Outlook Objects

Outlook provides a variety of ways for you to share objects including public folders, SharePoint servers, Meeting Workspace, and live attachments.

Creating a Public Folder

The first step in adding a public folder is to create a public folder tree. Follow the steps below.

1. Click on Start–Programs–Microsoft Exchange–System Manager.
2. Right-click on Folders, left-click on New, and then select Public Folder Tree.
3. Type the name of the new public folder tree in the name box.
4. Click on OK.

Now that you've added the public folder tree, you can create a public storage group for storage. You could also store it in an existing storage group. Follow these steps:

1. Click on Start–Programs–Microsoft Exchange–System Manager.
2. In the left section of the screen, double-click on Servers.
3. Right-click the server in which the new storage group should be created; click New and then Storage Group.
4. Type the name of the storage group in the Name box.
5. You can use the Zero Out Deleted Database Pages and Enable Circular Logging options for security and drive space considerations.
6. Click on OK to create the new storage group.

The final step in creating a new public folder is to create the new public folder store. Here's how.

1. Click on Start–Programs–Microsoft Exchange–System Manager.
2. In the left section of the screen, double-click on Servers.
3. Right-click the server in which the new storage group was created; click New and then Public Store.
4. Type the name of the public store in the Name box. It is best to use a name associated with the purpose. If incoming attachments are to be stored here, you should name it ATTACHMENTS.
5. Next to Associated Public Folder Store, click Browse. Notice that only the public folder tree that you created in the preceding section is shown.
6. Click on the public folder tree, and then click OK.
7. Click on the Database tab to set the locations of the database file (*.edb) and the streaming media files (*.stm).
8. You should configure the maintenance interval setting for the database to specify when online compaction runs. This procedure defragments the store but does not make it smaller.
9. Click OK to accept the changes.
10. Next click YES to mount the store immediately and make it available for public folders, and then click OK to finish.

Sharing Calendars and Contacts

One feature that was somewhat under-utilized in Outlook 2000 was the sharing capability of NetFolders. One calendar and/or set of contacts could be shared across a small office quite easily. There were some problems with NetFolders, but at least it worked most of the time. Because it was built into Outlook, it fit right in for small businesses and home users who had a need to share calendars and contacts.

There have been no sharing capabilities available (with Outlook alone) since the 2002 version. Some sharing options for the 2002 and 2003 versions are listed below.

> There is still a free method of sharing calendars and contacts through Outlook. These can be saved and e-mailed to other Outlook users. This method is a bit cumbersome and the data synchronization is handled manually, but it will work if the budget is really tight.

> A second (although slightly crippled) free option is the Microsoft Free/Busy service. This service is web-based and was previously explained in the Calendar section (see Setting Up the Microsoft Free/Busy Service on page 8-5).

> Exchange Server is one rather expensive option for sharing calendars and contacts between Outlook 2003 users. This works great with Outlook because Microsoft developed it. Exchange Server does an excellent job of handling e-mail, calendars, contacts, and more, and is recommended for larger installations.

> Web Publisher for Outlook allows you to share data through the web. It generates html pages from your Outlook calendar, contacts, tasks, and notes that can be uploaded to your own site or one of the many free services. The cost is $15 and you can download it from http://www.nightcreation.com/wpo/index.htm.

> CalShare allows uploading of Outlook shared appointments to their site. Users with appropriate permissions can then download the appointments into their calendars. All synchronization happens automatically after the user has signed up for their service and downloaded their add-in. Free as of 12/03. You can download it from http://www.pagethink.com/calshare.asp.

> Windows SharePoint Services (explained on the following page).

SharePoint Services

Windows SharePoint Services (WSS) provides a portal for collaboration among teams and team members. WSS is web-based, either through a company's Exchange Server connected to the web or one of the many WSS Hosting sites.

SharePoint Services work across many levels. These are:

➤ Team Community

- SharePoint sites provide places to capture and share ideas, information, communication, and documents. These allow team participation in discussions, shared documents, and surveys.
- Content can be accessed through a web browser and through Web Services clients.
- The ability to check documents in and out allows for complete and comprehensive document version control.

➤ Individual Empowerment

- Site members can find and communicate with key contacts and experts through e-mail and instant messaging.
- Site content is easily searched, and users can be alerted of existing document changes or newly added documents.
- Site content can be personalized on a per-user basis, even to the point of presenting targeted information to specific users.
- All of a site's collaborative content can be read and edited within Word® 2003, Excel® 2003, and PowerPoint® 2003.
- Outlook® 2003 allows SharePoint calendars to be viewed side-by-side with personal calendars.

➤ Management Enabler

- Site managers can customize the content and layout of sites. This ensures that site members can access and work with information relevant to them.
- Members' participation can also be monitored and moderated when necessary.
- Security and task responsibilities are both flexible and easily accessible.
- Well-designed lists and entire sites can be saved as templates. Individuals, teams, or business units can then reuse these templates across the entire organization.

➤ Administration and Deployment

- WSS can scale to thousands of sites within an organization.
- For site and server managers, quotas can be set and enforced on storage, sites per-server, and users per-site.
- Site usage can be monitored to detect and retire inactive sites.
- Detailed security options are available and easy to manage.
- Server managers can delegate the ability to create their own sites to the end-users.
- Sites and servers can be managed from a variety of tools: Web browser, command-line, or Web service-accessible object model.

Using Meeting Workspace

Meeting Workspace is a part of SharePoint Services. In an office environment, you can use Meeting Workspace to create a meeting invitation. This invitation is stored in a central area along with all information and materials associated with it.

To create a Meeting Workspace, click on Meeting Workspace when adding an appointment. This brings up one or more pages listing the items associated with a meeting. The typical meeting items are:

➤ Objectives

➤ Agenda

➤ Attendees

➤ Decisions

➤ Tasks

Additionally, document and picture libraries can be added where you can store materials related to the meeting. The lists and libraries depend on the template chosen when creating the Meeting Workspace.

Although the site is started from a template, it is totally customizable. Besides customizing appearance, you can modify the lists and libraries shown on the site.

Using Live Attachments

Live attachments are another feature of SharePoint Services. When a user sends a shared attachment, a Document Workspace site is created on the SharePoint Services site under that name.

The sender of a shared document is designated as the administrator of that Document Workspace site. All recipients of that attachment become "contributor" members of the site group.

If the attachment is a document from the 2003 versions of Word, Excel, PowerPoint, or Visio (or a Word or Excel XML file), the members can open and work on their own copy of the attachment. While the members are working on the attachment, the Document Workspace site occasionally updates the Office program in use. When finished, the changes can be saved to the Document Workspace copy.

Using Shortcut Panes

Another feature in Outlook 2003 is the Shortcut Pane. You can activate it by selecting the Shortcut icon (usually at the bottom of the navigation bar). ⊡

If the Shortcut icon is not displayed, you may need to configure the Navigation Pane to display it. Click on the arrow on the bottom right to begin.

Figure 9-17 Adding the Shortcut Icon

Using this option, buttons displayed on the Navigation Pane can be added or removed along with other configuration options.

The Shortcut Pane consists of "quick links" to any Outlook item of your choosing. Since there is such a great similarity between the Shortcut Pane and the Favorite Folders, we will not cover it in great detail here.

One extremely useful shortcut is to Outlook Update. Clicking here brings up the Office Update site in the View Pane and allows you to check the Update site for any new Outlook patches and updates that need to be installed.

Sending Internet Faxes

Using Outlook combined with an Internet faxing service, you can send faxes anywhere. This section briefly covers selecting an Internet faxing service and sending a fax.

Click File and then New. Now select Internet Fax. If you don't have an Internet fax service set up, Outlook presents you with an option to select a new provider. Click OK. The following web page displays in the default web browser.

Available Fax Services   Help

Fax Service Overview

Fax Services enable Microsoft Office 2003 customers to send and receive faxes over the Internet directly from within Office applications.

Available Fax Services

---

eFax provides faxing from all your Microsoft Office applications using your Internet connection. Incoming faxes arrive as e-mail attachments. Try it free for 30 days. Sign Up with eFax Fax Service *

Venali allows you to easily send and receive faxes right from Microsoft Office without the need for a fax machine or a separate fax line. Choose an area code for your individual fax number and receive faxes directly into your inbox, or send faxes from any Microsoft Office application right from your desktop with Venali. Try the service with a 30-day free trial. Sign Up with Venali Fax Service*

Figure 9-18 Available Fax Services Screen

Choose one of these services to install Internet faxing on your Outlook installation (the services listed may vary by area). It is beyond the scope of this book to detail setting up an Internet fax service, but the pricing is rather inexpensive for sending faxes anywhere in the US. The eFax service charges $12.95 per month and all received faxes are free. The charge on sent faxes is $ 0.10 per page within the US.

Of course, your system probably has a fax modem installed. If that is the case, it is already equipped for faxing documents. Couple the fax modem with a low-cost phone service and a dime per page begins to sound a bit expensive.

Using Smart Tags

Smart tags premiered in Outlook 2002 and provided a new level of integration between Office programs. There are many types of smart tags available with varying functionality. The general use of smart tags is to automatically bring information from one application to another. The built-in smart tag technology can perform actions based on the following:

> Addresses
> Dates
> Financial Symbols
> Names
> E-mail recipient names
> Places
> Telephone Numbers
> Times

If a smart tag is available, a dotted red line appears below the item and a smart tag symbol appears to the left of it once the mouse cursor is placed on the name. Date, telephone number, and name examples are shown below.

Date 1/16/04

Figure 9-19 Smart Tag

Clicking on the Date smart tag symbol produces this selection:

Figure 9-20 Date Smart Tag

The Telephone Number smart tag produces this selection:

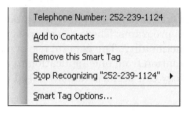

Figure 9-21 Telephone Number Smart Tag

And the Name smart tag produces this selection:

Figure 9-22 Name Smart Tag

Importing Data

Using Outlook, you can import from Internet Mail, Act, Lotus Organizer, Access, Excel, and many others. In this section, we will look at the procedure for importing contacts from an Excel file.

1. Click on File–Import and Export (see below). The Import and Export wizard launches and presents you with the screen in Figure 9-24.

Figure 9-23 File Menu, Importing and Exporting

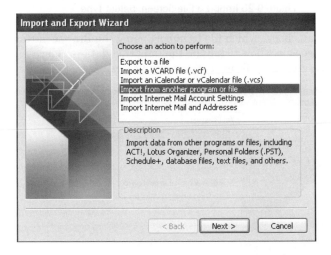

Figure 9-24 Import and Export Wizard Screen

2. Select Import from another program or file and click Next. You should see the Import a File screen shown below. Select the type of file you want to import. Click Next.

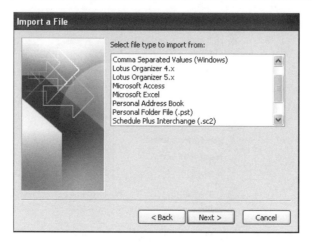

Figure 9-25 Import a File Screen, Select Type

3. Now you can choose which file to import using the Browse button. You can also select how to handle the imported data—replace duplicates, create duplicates, or skip duplicates.

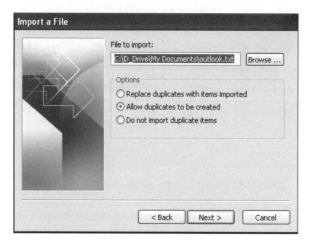

Figure 9-26 Import a File Screen, Select File

4. Next, choose which folder where you want to store the imported data.

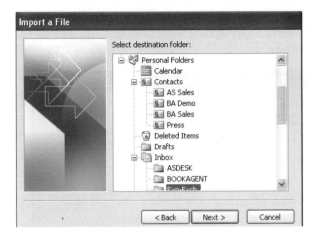

Figure 9-27 Import a File Screen, Select Destination

5. Check the option built by the wizard. Map the fields you are importing to the proper fields in Outlook.

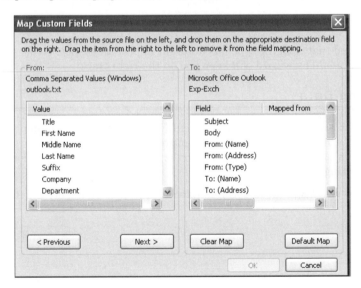

Figure 9-28 Mapping Imported Fields

6. Click OK to finish the import procedure. The final Import a File
    screen displays to verify exactly what is being performed by the
    import procedure.

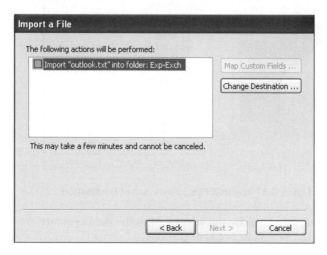

Figure 9-29 Map Custom Fields Screen

Keep in mind that each file type has different import and export steps
and procedures. The wizard will keep you on the right track.

Exporting Data

You can also export to quite a few different formats. The most commonly
supported format for importing into other programs will be comma-
separated values. Below is the process for exporting along with a portion
of the resulting file.

1. Start by selecting File–Import and Export. Then click on Export to a file.

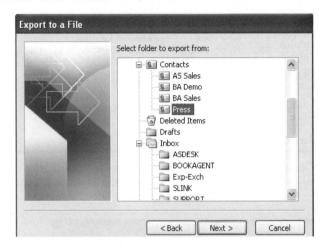

Figure 9-30 Export to a File Screen, Select Folder

2. Select the folder from the list above. Outlook then prompts you to name the file to export to.

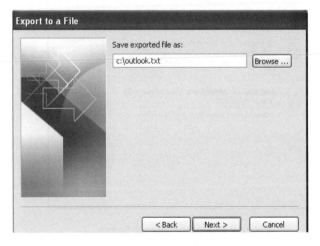

Figure 9-31 Export to a File Screen, Select Destination

Below you see the first few items of an exported contacts list. They are in tab-delimited format. This means there is a tab between each separate field. This is the most common format to use for exporting to almost any program.

```
"WITN Channel 7","","","PO Box 468",,,"Washington","NC","27889"
"WCTI TV12","","","PO Box 12325",,,"New Bern","NC","28561","Uni
"WNCT TV9","","","P.O. Box 898",,,"Greenville","NC","27835","Un
"UPN TV48","","","3500 Myer Lee Drive",,,"Winston-Salem","NC","
"WNCN TV17","","","1205 Front Street",,,"Raleigh","N.C.","27609
","","","WTVD TV11","","","411 Liberty Street",,,"Durham","NC",
"WRAZ TV50","","","P.O. Box 30050",,,"Durham","NC","27702-3050"
```

Figure 9-32 Excerpt from Exported Contacts List

Using the Mailbox Cleanup Wizard

The Mailbox Cleanup Wizard is a very useful utility for cleaning unnecessary items out of your mailbox. To access the Mailbox Cleanup Wizard, click on Tools–Mailbox Cleanup.

Figure 9-33 Mailbox Cleanup Screen

Clicking the Empty button in the Mailbox Cleanup screen empties your Deleted Items folder. The View Mailbox Size button lets you view the size of each individual folder (and sub-folders, if they exist). It might seem to be improperly named because it actually allows you to view the size of not only your Contacts folder, but that of other folders, as well. See the following figure.

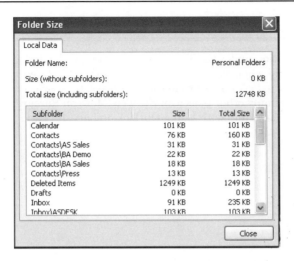

Figure 9-34 Folder Size Screen

The second section in the Mailbox Cleanup screen lets you find items older than xx number of days, larger than xx size, or using just about any other characteristic. Click on Find–Advanced Find to configure your search using the Messages, More Choices, and Advanced tabs.

Figure 9-35 Advanced Find Screen

AutoArchive, which is in the third section, lets you move older items to the Archive folder. You can set up the autoarchiving properties on individual mailboxes so that they will happen every xx number of days.

Using Research

Research is an option under the Tools menu for Mail, Calendar, Contacts, Tasks, and Journal whenever the cursor is in a text field. Research gives you the capability to look up a word in the dictionary, thesaurus, translations, and many other places on the web. More on Research Tools in later chapters (see Help with Using Outlook on page 10-1 and Parental Controls on page 12-3).

10. Help with Using Outlook

Outlook has different kinds of help available. In this section we will go over their advantages and disadvantages.

The first help option we'll cover is the "old" style of help that you accessed from the Help menu in the menu bar. Click Help and Microsoft Office Outlook Help (or press the F1 key) and the screen shown below appears.

Figure 10-1 Outlook Help Screen

Type the desired search word or phrase in the Search for box. Click on the green arrow to start your search, which will be done online if you are connected to the Internet. Different types of documents will be returned in a window. Some of these are explained below.

This symbol appears beside help that is available from the standard help system. This type of help does not require an Internet connection.

This symbol displays if the destination is an online Office web page.

Clicking on this symbol loads an article from Microsoft Office Online.

The help displayed beside this symbol leads to a training link on Microsoft Online.

Other Places To Look will be displayed at the bottom of the Help window. These include:

> Clip art and media
> Get answers from other users
> Research
> Knowledge Base Search

Clicking on one of these expands the search beyond the usual Microsoft help areas and gives the opportunity to learn more on the subject from many differing areas.

The Search bar is at the bottom of the Help window.

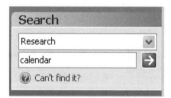

Figure 10-2 - Search Bar

It adds the capability to search for a word or phrase in any of the following areas:

> Microsoft Office Online
> Assistance
> Training
> Offline Help
> Clip Art and Media
> Office Marketplace
> Research

Using the Office Assistant

You can also access Help through the Office Assistant. If the Office Assistant is not displayed, click on Help and then Show The Office Assistant. The robot (his name is F1) is shown below.

Figure 10-3 Office Assistant Initial Screen

All assistants show this yellow box when you click them on. Type a word or phrase and the same Help Pane already shown will appear (see Figure 10-1). You can change the Office Assistant to one of many different characters and "personalities."

Access the screen shown below by right-clicking on the Office Assistant and selecting Properties.

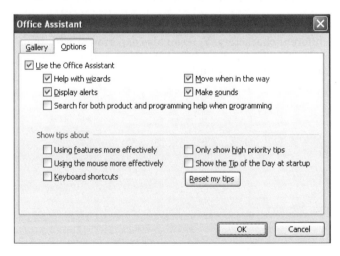

Figure 10-4 Office Assistant Right-click Options

Use this screen to configure the help system to suit your varying needs and wishes.

Notice that the Show Tips About selections are all unselected. If you check one or more of these, Outlook will display a tip each time it starts.

Click on the Gallery tab on this screen to change the Office Assistant to another character.

If you don't see the office assistant on your screen, you can click on Help-Show the Office Assistant and it should appear.

 There are multiple office assistants available in Office. The default is the paper clip. His name is Clippit.

 Another is the Dot.

 To the left you see a nifty little robot whose name is F1. Maybe he is named after the ever-helpful F1 key.

 If you occasionally like a little magic you can choose Merlin as your office assistant.

 If you like animals, you can choose Links the cat or Rocky the dog. Just like your friends or the family pet, each assistant has its own personality and actions.

 Play around with your office assistant by selecting different characters. You can also experiment with them by right-clicking on each and choosing Animate. They do some really funny stuff!!

11. Macros: Automating Outlook

Outlook can be programmed to automatically do many things from a variety of different programs. These include Visual Basic, Visual FoxPro, Visual C, Delphi, Word, PowerPoint, and the list stretches as far as your imagination.

This "open architecture" is due to something called the Outlook Object Model, which presents you with five automation projects. The first three use other programs in conjunction with Outlook to accomplish the task. The last two are completely within Outlook. They are:

> Create a new contact and insert the various pieces of information from fields entered in a Word document

> Create a merged document and e-mail using Outlook and Microsoft Word

> Send a custom HTML-formatted E-mail using an Excel spreadsheet

> Automatically save attachments from a certain sender

> "Explode" an e-mail into multiple e-mails

If you are interested in utilizing Outlook to the fullest extent, you should find this section to be quite interesting.

Creating a New Contact from Word

First, we will create the Word document that holds our contact information. Within Microsoft Word, create a document with the fields you see below.

```
First Name:
Middle Initial:
Last Name:
Company:
Address:
City, St Zip:
Phone:
Fax:
Cell:
E-mail1:
E-mail2:
Web Page:
Category:
```

Now assign bookmarks to the data entered into these fields. You can do this by putting the cursor at the point where the bookmark is to be inserted, clicking on the Insert menu, and then on Bookmark. Name the bookmark, click on Add, and you're done.

The next step is to enter the macro to create a new contact and fill in the information. In the Word document, click on Tools–Macro–Macros and click on the Create button. Enter the following code in a blank spot above any Sub or below any End Sub commands that are already there.

```
Sub CreateNewContact()
    ' these four commands are required to set up the
    ' variables necessary for creating a new Outlook instance
    Dim oOutlook As Outlook.Application
    Dim oMAPI As Outlook.NameSpace
    Dim oFolder As Outlook.MAPIFolder
    Dim oContactItem As Outlook.ContactItem
    ' necessary for error control
    On Error Resume Next
    ' create the new Outlook instance
    Set oOutlook = New Outlook.Application
    ' verify that it was created properly
    If Not oOutlook Is Nothing Then
      ' Get the MAPI NameSpace object
      Set oMAPI = oOutlook.Session
      ' verify that it was created properly
      If Not oMAPI Is Nothing Then
        ' Log in to the MAPI session
        oMAPI.Logon , , True, True
        ' Create a pointer to the Contact folder
        Set oFolder = oMAPI.GetDefaultFolder(olFolderContact)
        ' verify that it was created properly
        If Not oFolder Is Nothing Then
          ' Create a new item in the Contact folder
          Set oContactItem = oFolder.Items.Add(olContactItem)
          ' verify that it was created properly
          If Not oContactItem Is Nothing Then
            With oContactItem
              ' fill the contact fields from the bookmarked
              ' Word fields
              .FirstName =
ActiveDocument.Bookmarks("first").Range.Text
              .LastName =
ActiveDocument.Bookmarks("last").Range.Text
              .MiddleName =
ActiveDocument.Bookmarks("mi").Range.Text
              .CompanyName = _
ActiveDocument.Bookmarks("company").Range.Text
              .HomeAddress = _
ActiveDocument.Bookmarks("addr").Range.Text & vbCrLf &  _
ActiveDocument.Bookmarks("csz").Range.Text
              .HomeTelephoneNumber = _
```

```
ActiveDocument.Bookmarks("phone").Range.Text
            .HomeFaxNumber = _
ActiveDocument.Bookmarks("fax").Range.Text
            .MobileTelephoneNumber = _
ActiveDocument.Bookmarks("cell").Range.Text
            .E-mail1Address = _ ActiveDocument.Bookmarks("e-
mail1").Range.Text
            .E-mail2Address = _ ActiveDocument.Bookmarks("e-
mail2").Range.Text
            .WebPage =
ActiveDocument.Bookmarks("web").Range.Text
            .Categories =
ActiveDocument.Bookmarks("cat").Range.Text
            ' save the contact item
            .Save
            ' clean up the variables set
            Set oContactItem = Nothing
          End With
        End If
        Set oFolder = Nothing
      End If
      oMAPI.Logoff
    End If
    Set oMAPI = Nothing
  End If
  Set oOutlook = Nothing
End Sub
```

The rather lengthy macro above takes the bookmarks created in the Word document and places them in the corresponding fields in the new contact it creates. The underscore (_) character indicates that the next line is to be typed on the same line.

For example, E-mail2Address = ActiveDocument.Bookmarks... should be typed on a single line of the macro editor. The lines that start with a hyphen (') are considered comments. These can contain anything you want as long as the hyphen is the first character in the line.

The macro was created and run in Word 2003, but should work well in Word 2000 and above. The contact it created was in Outlook 2003. It should also work for Outlook 2000 and above.

Creating E-mail Merges

In this section we will create a merge document that will be initiated in Outlook and finished in Word. In order to provide the broadest experience, we will merge the document to a new document (which can be printed and/or saved) and then merged to e-mail.

If you want to select only specific contacts and/or fields to process in this merge, click on the View menu. Then select Arrange By–Current View– Customize Current View. This allows you to set a filter for only selected records and also to select specific fields to be displayed.

Follow the steps below to prepare Outlook for merging:

1. Select Contacts within Outlook.
2. Click on the Tools menu.
3. Click on Mail Merge (you may need to place your mouse cursor over the two arrows at the bottom to make all menu options visible).

The Mail Merge Contacts screen lets you select whether to use all contacts or only those in the view. The same goes for the fields selected— you can use all fields or only those selected in the View.

The Document file section of this screen lets you choose the destination as a new document or as an existing document. For instance, if you had previously defined a document and wanted to re-use it, then you would choose Existing Document. Normally, though, you will want to select New Document.

You can use the Contact data file section to store the data being used in a permanent data file. For example, if you want to select only certain records from a large contact list, you would find this option to be quite handy.

The Merge options section is where you choose the document type and destination. Although you may have chosen E-mail, the merge will still be performed in Microsoft Word.

In the Mail Merge Contacts screen, make the following selections:

➢ All contacts in current view
➢ Contact fields in current view
➢ New Document
➢ Permanent file is unchecked
➢ Document Type: Form Letters
➢ Merge To: New Document

After clicking on the OK button, a screen similar to that pictured below will pop up if you have Microsoft Word 2003 installed.

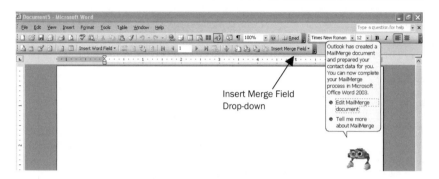

Figure 11-1 Mail Merge Document in Word

Notice that on the lower toolbar to the right is a drop-down labeled Insert Merge Field. This is a requirement for easily setting up a merge document. When you click on that drop-down, you will be presented with the list of the fields are available for merging.

Tip: If you want a tutorial on merging with Word, you can click on the Tell me more button.

Merging to a Form Letter

You type a form letter merge document just like you would a normal business letter. Perform the following steps to create the document shown on the following page.

1. Drop down Insert Merge Field and select Full Name. Press the ENTER key.
2. Select Company from the drop down. Press ENTER
3. Select Mailing Address, then press ENTER twice. This will provide the street address, city, state, and zip, already formatted.
4. Type in Dear and a space. Now select First Name and then type a colon (:) after it. Press ENTER twice.
5. Type in whatever you want to appear in this letter. The sample letter here will make a business proposition and will close with a statement that they will be contacted at their phone number in about a week.

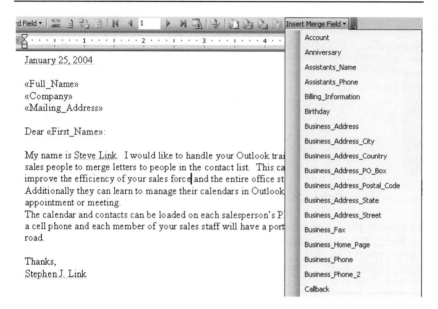

Figure 11-2 Mail Merge Letter

Notice the date in the upper left corner of the merge document. I placed the date there by using the Insert menu and selecting Date and Time. Using this feature ensures that the current date prints each time you merge this letter.

The fields inside of the brackets <<>> are merge fields that I selected from the Insert Merge Fields drop down (shown here also).

Each field will be filled with the corresponding entry from the contact record to create a letter that appears like the following example.

December 12, 2003

Mr. Cliff Clementine
Eastern Assoc
413 Bunting Hue Dr
Jacksonville, NC 28765

Dear Cliff:

My name is Steve Link. I would like to handle your training in Outlook. I can train your sales people to merge their sales documents, manage sales contacts, and never miss a meeting due to the magnificent scheduling capabilities of Outlook.

I will call you at (252) 239-1124 within a week to discuss this proposal.

Thanks,
Steve Link

I created this letter by clicking on the Merge to New Document button.

Figure 11-3 Merge to New Document button

If you select a contact list with five hundred contacts, the end result will be the same form letter merged with the information from each contact.

Merging to E-mail

Merging to e-mail is also a possibility. You can generate an e-mail merge by clicking on the Merge to E-mail button, which is two over from the Merge to New Document button. This produces an e-mail with the same information. Outlook presents you with the following screen after you click on the Merge to E-mail button.

Figure 11-4 Merge to E-mail Screen

E-mail is the default in the To line. Sending to a fax number is also an option if the proper faxing software is installed. Enter the subject here, along with selecting from HTML, attachment, or plain text as the mail format.

The bottom section affords you the ability to select only certain records to use for merging.

Merging Custom E-mail from Excel

In this section we will create an Excel spreadsheet with first name, last name, e-mail address, e-mail login ID, and two other fields. First I'll show you the layout of the Excel spreadsheet. Following that are the macros you need to type into the VBA Editor in Excel; the final thing you'll see is one of the e-mails I created.

The Excel spreadsheet should have headers in the first row with data following that. The data columns are defined by their names (First Name, Last Name, E-mail address, ISP ID). The next column determines whether or not to send the e-mail to this person (put a YES if this person is to receive the e-mail). The last column displays the results of the send. The spreadsheet layout is on the following page.

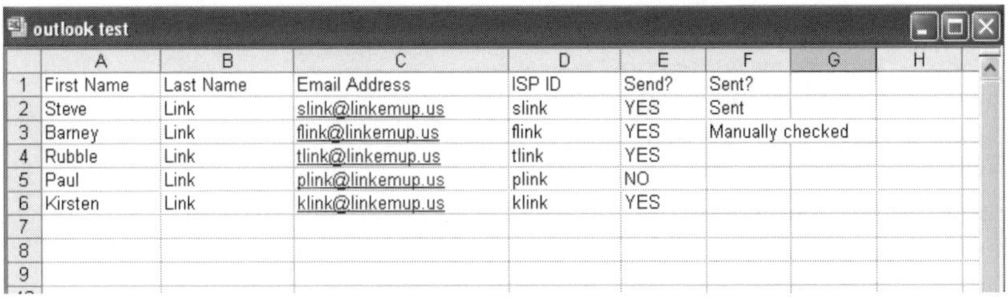

	A	B	C	D	E	F	G	H
1	First Name	Last Name	Email Address	ISP ID	Send?	Sent?		
2	Steve	Link	slink@linkemup.us	slink	YES	Sent		
3	Barney	Link	flink@linkemup.us	flink	YES	Manually checked		
4	Rubble	Link	tlink@linkemup.us	tlink	YES			
5	Paul	Link	plink@linkemup.us	plink	NO			
6	Kirsten	Link	klink@linkemup.us	klink	YES			
7								
8								
9								

Figure 11-5 Excel Spreadsheet

Notice that we want to send to all but one address and that the first two have already been sent. If the macro does not see anything in the F (Sent?) column it, it will send the e-mail as long as there is a YES in the E (Send?) column. If there is something in the F column or NO in the E column, then it skips that address. The macros are below.

```
Option Explicit
Dim olApp As Outlook.Application
Dim the-mail As Outlook.MailItem


Function set_body(displayName As String, ISPAccount As String)
_ As String

set_body = "<html>"
set_body = set_body & "<head>"
set_body = set_body & "<meta http-equiv='Content-Type'
content='text/html; charset=windows-1252'>"
set_body = set_body & "<meta name='GENERATOR'
content='Microsoft FrontPage 4.0'>"
set_body = set_body & "<meta name='ProgId'
content='FrontPage.Editor.Document'>"
set_body = set_body & "<title>New Page 1</title>"
set_body = set_body & "</head>"
set_body = set_body & "<body>"
set_body = set_body & "<div><font face='Verdana'>To the
attention of: <b>" & displayName & "</b></font><br>"
set_body = set_body & "  <font face='Verdana'> Your"
set_body = set_body & "  ISP account: <font
color='#FF0000'><b>(" & ISPAccount & ")</b></font>"
set_body = set_body & "  </font>"
set_body = set_body & "</div>"
set_body = set_body & "<div>"
set_body = set_body & "   "
```

```
set_body = set_body & "</div>"
set_body = set_body & "<div>"
set_body = set_body & "  "
set_body = set_body & "</div>"
set_body = set_body & "<div>"
set_body = set_body & " <font face='Verdana'>According to _
the"
set_body = set_body & " ISP billing system you have not _
used your ISP account"
set_body = set_body & " since January 1st, 2003.</font>"
set_body = set_body & "</div>"
set_body = set_body & "<div>"
set_body = set_body & "  "
set_body = set_body & "</div>"
set_body = set_body & "<div>"
set_body = set_body & " <font face='Verdana'><strong>We _
would like you"
set_body = set_body & " to confirm by return e-mail that you _
have a regular use of it</strong>, <strong>otherwise"
set_body = set_body & " <font color=#ff0000>your ISP _ account
will be deactivated on May 31st, _ 2003</font></strong> as
we "
set_body = set_body & " cannot afford to keep wasting _
money on unused subscriptions.</font>"
set_body = set_body & "</div>"
set_body = set_body & "<div>"
set_body = set_body & "  "
set_body = set_body & "</div>"
set_body = set_body & "<div>"
set_body = set_body & "  "
set_body = set_body & "</div>"
set_body = set_body & "<div>"
set_body = set_body & "  "
set_body = set_body & "</div>"
set_body = set_body & "<div>"
set_body = set_body & " <font face='Verdana' size='2'>Note: _
<u>Alternative"
set_body = set_body & " solutions to accessing mail and _
Intranet</u><font color='#0000ff'></font></font>"
set_body = set_body & "</div>"
set_body = set_body & "<div>"
set_body = set_body & "  "
set_body = set_body & "</div>"
```

```
set_body = set_body & "<div>"
set_body = set_body & "  <font face='Verdana' size='2' _
color='#0000ff'><u>Using"
set_body = set_body & "  CGG laptop: </u> </font>"
set_body = set_body & "</div>"
set_body = set_body & "<div>"
set_body = set_body & "  <ul>"
set_body = set_body & "    <li><font face='Verdana' _
size='2'>Most"
set_body = set_body & "      of the processing centers and _
agencies are now connected to our"
set_body = set_body & "      network thus allowing you to _
access your mailbox through either Outlook or"
set_body = set_body & "      Webmail (requires a specific _
authorization).</font></li>"
set_body = set_body & "  </ul>"
set_body = set_body & "</div>"
set_body = set_body & "<div>"
set_body = set_body & "  <ul>"
set_body = set_body & "    <li><font face='Verdana' size='2'>_
A fairly"
set_body = set_body & "      large number of you already have _
a DSL or a cable Internet access at home"
set_body = set_body & "      on which SecureRemote (VPN) can _
be used to access our internal network"
set_body = set_body & "      (requires a SecurID _
card)</font></li>"
set_body = set_body & "  </ul>"
set_body = set_body & "</div>"
set_body = set_body & "<div>"
set_body = set_body & "  <ul>"
set_body = set_body & "    <li><font face='Verdana' _
size='2'>Some"
set_body = set_body & "      countries such as France have free
_ Internet access (freesurf, free, ...),"
set_body = set_body & "      on which SecureRemote (VPN) can _
be used to access our internal network"
set_body = set_body & "      (requires a SecurID _
card)</font></li>"
set_body = set_body & "  </ul>"
set_body = set_body & "</div>"
set_body = set_body & "<div>"
set_body = set_body & "  <ul>"
```

```
set_body = set_body & "    <li><font face='Verdana' _
size='2'>Some"
set_body = set_body & "      countries such as MiddleEast have
_ only a local ISP offering (i.e."
set_body = set_body & "      ISP is not working) on which _
SecureRemote (VPN) can be used to"
set_body = set_body & "      access our internal network _
(requires a SecurID card)</font></li>"
set_body = set_body & "  </ul>"
set_body = set_body & "</div>"
set_body = set_body & "<div>"
set_body = set_body & "  <ul>"
set_body = set_body & "    <li><font face='Verdana' _
size='2'>Some"
set_body = set_body & "      countries such as South America _
are better served by ATT than by"
set_body = set_body & "      ISP (some of you have already an _
ATT account)</font></li>"
set_body = set_body & "  </ul>"
set_body = set_body & "</div>"
set_body = set_body & "<div>"
set_body = set_body & "  <font face='Verdana' color='#0000ff' _
size='2'><u>Without"
set_body = set_body & "  CGG PC:</u></font>"
set_body = set_body & "</div>"
set_body = set_body & "<div>"
set_body = set_body & "  <font face='Verdana' size='2'>And _
finally, we"
set_body = set_body & "  are in the process of opening the _
access to a Webmail and intranet access"
set_body = set_body & "  from any Internet access (cybercaf's,
_ hotels, hot-spots, ...), you will only"
set_body = set_body & "  need to carry your SecuriD card and _
remember your e-mail aliasname and"
set_body = set_body & "  domain.</font>"
set_body = set_body & "</div>"
set_body = set_body & "<div>"
set_body = set_body & "   "
set_body = set_body & "</div>"
set_body = set_body & "<div>"
set_body = set_body & "   "
set_body = set_body & "</div>"
set_body = set_body & "<div>"
```

```
set_body = set_body & "  <font _
face='Verdana'>Regards,</font>"
set_body = set_body & "</div>"
set_body = set_body & "<div>"
set_body = set_body & "   "
set_body = set_body & "</div>"
set_body = set_body & "<div>"
set_body = set_body & "  <font face='Verdana' size='2'>"
set_body = set_body & "  <div>"
set_body = set_body & "    <font face='Verdana' color=_
'#000080' size='2'><strong>IT Security</strong></font>"
set_body = set_body & "  </div>"
set_body = set_body & "  </font>"
set_body = set_body & "</div>"
set_body = set_body & "</body>"
set_body = set_body & "</html>"

End Function
'----------------------------------------

Sub sendMail_click()
Dim SafeItem As Object

Dim i As Integer
Dim nr As Integer
Dim accISP As String
Dim dispN As String
Dim olExist As Boolean
Dim e-mailN As String

Dim olApp As Outlook.Application

    olExist = True
    On Error Resume Next
    Set olApp = GetObject(, "Outlook.Application")

    If Err.Number <> 0 Then
        olExist = False
        Err.Clear
        On Error Resume Next
        If Not IsEmpty(olApp) Then
            Set olApp = CreateObject("Outlook.Application")
        End If
```

```
        If Err.Number <> 0 Then
            Err.Clear
            MsgBox "Cant start Outlook", vbCritical, "Error"
            Exit Sub
        End If
    End If
    'olApp.Visible = True
    nr = ActiveSheet.UsedRange.Rows.Count
    For i = 2 To nr
        If Cells(i, 5).Value = "YES" And Cells(i, 6).Value = ""
Then
            dispN = Cells(i, 2).Value & ", " & Cells(i,
1).Value
            accISP = Cells(i, 4).Value
            If Cells(i, 3).Value = "" Then
                e-mailN = Cells(i, 2).Value & ", " & Cells(i,
1)
            Else
                e-mailN = Cells(i, 3).Value
            End If
'            Set SafeItem = _ CreateObject("Redemption.Safe-
mailItem") 'Create an instance of _ Redemption.Safe-mailItem
            Set the-mail = olApp.CreateItem(olMailItem) 'Create
a _ new message
'            SafeItem.Item = the-mail 'set Item property
            the-mail.Recipients.Add dispN
            the-mail.Recipients.ResolveAll
            the-mail.HTMLBody = set_body(dispN, accISP)
            the-mail.Subject = "Your ISP account (" & accISP &
")"
            If the-mail.Recipients.ResolveAll Then
                the-mail.Send
                Cells(i, 6).Value = "Sent"
            Else
                the-mail.Display True
                Cells(i, 6).Value = "Manually checked"
            End If

            Set the-mail = Nothing
            Set SafeItem = Nothing

        End If
```

```
    Next

    If olExist = False Then
        olApp.Application.Quit
        Set olApp = Nothing
    End If
End Sub
```

Notice that the set SafeItem = ... and the SafeItem.Item = ... lines are commented out. This is required if your system has an add-in called Redemption. If you have installed Redemption, then the lines following those that have the-mail.Recipients (or similar text) would need to be changed to SafeItem.Recipients. This occurs seven times in the macro above.

The Send_Mail function is the routine that actually handles sending the mail. It looks at rows two and below (one is the header) and processes the mail according to the cell contents.

Send_Mail resolves the e-mail address based on your Contacts list. If it finds a contact by the first and last names you entered, it uses that e-mail address and places the word SENT in column F. If it does not find the names, Send_Mail prompts you to enter a valid e-mail address and click Send. It then places Manually Checked in column F.

The Set_Body function creates the HTML-formatted e-mail. This function contains HTML "commands" that control the formatting (fonts, colors) of the e-mail to be sent. This could be changed to Set_Body = "Test E-mail" if you prefer to create a much simpler e-mail. A portion of the E-mail created for Kirsten Link is shown below.

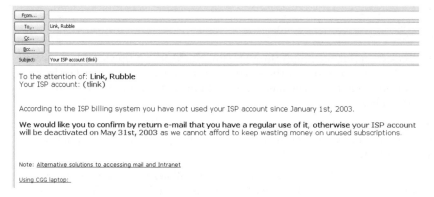

Figure 11-6 Resulting E-mail

Automatically Saving Attachments

This macro automatically saves any attachments from a certain sender to the hard drive. It is important to keep in mind that it should not be run for all e-mail. You could automatically save a virus attachment or something else that could be quite destructive.

Within Outlook, click on Tools–Macro–Visual Basic Editor (or Alt+F11). You will be presented with (basically) a blank screen. Click on Insert and then Module in order to copy this macro and save it. The macro code is below.

```
Sub saverep()
    Dim oApp As Application 'set up the variables
    Dim oNS As NameSpace
    Dim oMessage As Object
    Dim oAttachments As Outlook.Attachments
    Dim NbrMsgs

    ' Create new Outlook application
    Set oApp = New Outlook.Application
    Set oNS = oApp.GetNamespace("MAPI")
    Set oFolder = oNS.GetDefaultFolder(olFolderInbox)
    NbrMsgs = 0
    ' Cycle through the messages
    For Each oMessage In oFolder.Items
        With oMessage
            If .SenderName = "TheBoss" Then
                NbrMsgs = NbrMsgs + 1
                oMessage.Attachments.Item(1).SaveAsFile_
                    "C:\reports\in\" & NbrMsgs & "report.txt"
                .Delete
            End If
        End With
    Next
End Sub
```

The lines from Sub saverep() through Dim NbrMsgs set up variables needed for use in the rest of the program. Set oApp creates a new Outlook application in memory. The messages that follow it set up functions to open the inbox.

The active part of this macro is the loop through each message in the inbox and the processing of the attachment (if any). This is accomplished with the For Each ... Next loop.

The line below For Each allows the code that follows it to examine the contents of the message. The next line checks to see if the sender name is TheBoss. It will look for attachments only in messages sent from TheBoss.

NbrMsgs is incremented to separate one attachment from the next. Notice that it is used in the file name (which is the line below it). The line that actually saves the attachment is next. It is saved in the C:\REPORTS\IN directory and is saved as 1report.txt, 2report.txt, etc.

The next line deletes the message after processing. The final four lines are closing lines for their counterparts (If...Endif, With...End With, For...Next, Sub...End Sub).

Exploding an E-mail

This macro creates a number of e-mails from one single e-mail message. As it is written, the addresses would be placed in the BCC field. To have them placed in the CC field, simply replace "Bcc" with "Cc". The macro code is below.

```
Public Sub explode-mail()
' assuming code is running in outlook 2000/2002s
' vba environment
Dim Bccs() As String
Dim nBccs As Integer
Dim i As Integer
Dim colSelection As Outlook.Selection
Dim oMessage As Outlook.MailItem
Dim colObj As Object
Set colSelection = Application.ActiveExplorer.Selection
If colSelection.Count = 0 Then
    Set colSelection = Nothing
    Exit Sub
End If
For Each colObj In colSelection
    Bccs = Split(colObj.BCC, ";", -1)
    nBccs = UBound(Bccs)
    For i = 0 To nBccs
        Set oMessage = colObj.Copy
        oMessage.BCC = ""
        oMessage.To = Bccs(i)
        oMessage.HTMLBody = colObj.HTMLBody
'       comment this line out after testing is complete
        oMessage.Display True
'       UNcomment this line after testing is complete
            'oMessage.Send
    Next
Next
Set colSelection = Nothing
End Sub
```

The colSelection variable stores the entire message. If there is no message when the macro runs, it exits per the Exit Sub line.

The first For Each ... Next loop breaks the addresses in the BCC field apart.

The second For Each ... Next loop creates a new e-mail with the same body and puts the address into the TO field. There are actually two lines that work with the e-mail in this loop. The first is

```
oMessage.Display True
```

This line displays the message and allows you to click Send before sending it. With this line in place, you will actually have to send fifty e-mails if you have that many addresses in the BCC field. The other line that handles the e-mail is

```
'oMessage.Send
```

Notice the apostrophe (') in front of this line. That means it is currently commented out and will not execute. The comments at the end of these two lines give the reasoning behind this. Test the macro first with Display implemented to see how it works. If you are happy with it, you can comment the Display line and remove the comment character on the Send line.

The macro, as it is designed, sends the message to each address in the BCC field. It creates a new e-mail for each one and places that address in the To field of the new message.

Keep Outlook security in mind when running this or any macro. It might pop up with each e-mail and it could disable running macros altogether. To get around an inability to run macros, take the following steps within Outlook.

1. Click on Tools.
2. Hover over Macro.
3. Click on Security.
4. Select Medium or Low.

Do not forget to set the security back when you are finished with it. Leaving the security setting at a lower setting could expose your computer to the many viruses and Trojans that are out on the World Wide Web.

As stated above, this macro, as currently written, will place the addresses in the BCC field. You can change the addresses to the TO field by changing the line

```
Bccs = Split(colObj.BCC, ";", -1)
```

to

```
Bccs = Split(colObj.TO, ";", -1)
```

Tip: This macro will not run as written with Word as the e-mail editor. That option is located under the Tools menu. Click on Options and then the Mail Format tab. Uncheck the Use Word 2003 checkbox.

This page intentionally left blank.

12. Safe E-mailing

Protecting Against Spam and Viruses

Do you really enjoy the large amount of unsolicited e-mail that comes into your Inbox? Most likely not. There are specific methods and procedures that you can use to avoid wasting time on spam. We'll cover a few of those here along with some web sites you can review for more suggestions.

Outlook 2003 includes an easy method to get rid of spam that works quite well—Junk E-mail rules. As previously mentioned, these can be locked down to the point of accepting e-mail only from a specified list of senders or domains.

This method may be effective and useful in a business environment, but it means modifying the list of approved senders every time a new contact is going to send you an e-mail.

Note: Blocked Senders was covered in detail previously (see Right-click E-mail Menu Options on page 8-50). After you receive an e-mail for the first time, adding a new sender or domain to this list is only a right-click away.

The main focus of this section is keeping unwanted e-mail from being received at all. By modifying the Send/Receive settings to download headers only (mentioned on page 9-14), Outlook will not download the offending (and sometimes large) e-mail. This will decrease the amount of time required to retrieve your e-mail. Just delete the obvious spam (based on the header) and then download the other messages.

Another option for blocking the spam from ever being downloaded is called a spam filter. Your Internet provider may have one of these content-based filters installed. If properly set up, spam filters work well. The best use for these filters is to add a header to the potential spam message and subject. This gives the recipient a chance to decide if the message is truly spam. The reasoning behind this is that the filter may mark desired e-mail as spam and block it at the server. This has happened with automatically generated news messages.

A search of the web provides the following links regarding spam filtering (plus many more):

    A Plan For Spam - www.paulgraham.com/spam.html

    Spam Assassin - www.spamassassin.org

```
Spam Bouncer - www.spambouncer.org

The Spam Filter - www.scot.demon.co.uk/spam-filter.html
```

Virus protection is something else that should be installed on the Internet provider's server. Most of these scanners will check an e-mail once it is received. If it contains a known virus, the intended recipient will receive an e-mail containing the name of the virus and who sent it. The e-mail (and virus) itself is destroyed so that it can't infect anyone.

You should not leave virus protection entirely up to someone else, though. If a virus comes into your system and wipes out years of work that was always supposed to be backed up next week, it could be disastrous.

Purchase a virus protection package and install it as an extra hedge against a virus infection. Verify that it protects the computer by scanning files for known viruses and that it also scans incoming e-mails.

Some packages are free and some are not. A few are listed below. The first three are free for personal use.

```
Trend Micro - housecall.antivirus.com

Symantec - security.symantec.com

AVG - www.grisoft.com

Symantec Norton Antivirus - www.symantec.com

Network Associates McAffee - www.nai.com
```

A search on your favorite search engine will list many different virus protection programs. The most effective approach to virus protection is to use multiple pieces of software and hope the second will catch anything missed by the first. For example, install Norton Antivirus and do a monthly scan at the Trend Micro housecall site to ensure that nothing was missed by the installed software.

Blocking External HTML

Another hedge against allowing viruses and spy programs onto your computer is to enable External HTML Blocking.

To change these settings, click on Tools, Options, and then the Security tab. Now click on the Change Automatic Download Settings button. As shown in the screen shot below, the default is to have all of these checked. This is the most secure setting.

Figure 12-1 Automatic Picture Download Settings

The best recommendation is to leave all of these checked. Yes, it is a bit inconvenient to click the extra button to download pictures from your EBay searches or your friend's e-mailed newsletter. But it is a much bigger inconvenience (and quite costly) to get rid of a nasty virus that has infected your system because your security was low enough to allow it in.

Parental Controls

The newly implemented Research Library is a useful tool. It allows easy gathering of information from a huge number of prestigious resources. Although informative, some of the content may not be suitable for young children.

If young children are using this installation of Outlook, it may be a good idea to implement parental controls on the Research Library. To modify the parental controls, open a new e-mail and click on Tools and Research. In the Research Pane, you'll find a Research Options link at the bottom. Click on that to bring up a screen that allows you to select and deselect the reference sources. This screen also has a Parental Controls button on it. Clicking on it produces the following screen.

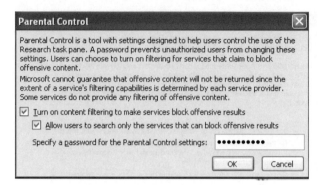

Figure 12-2 Parental Control Screen

Check the Turn on content filtering ... box and set a password. Now the services will automatically block results that they consider offensive.

Digital Certificates

In today's world of e-mail viruses and identity theft, many people are turning to digital certificates (or Digital ID) as a method of proving that the sender is actually who he/she claims to be. In this section, we will go through the process of requesting a Digital ID and configuring Outlook to use it.

Click on Tools, Options, and the Security tab. Now click on the Get a Digital ID button. The default web browser will open up with a few links, which starts the process of acquiring a Digital ID. That screen is shown below.

Available digital IDs

  VeriSign provides digital IDs for secure e-mail. Use your VeriSign digital ID to digitally sign e-mail messages, assuring recipients that your e-mail messages really came from you and not an impostor. You can also use your digital ID to encrypt the contents of your messages (including attachments), letting recipients know that your e-mail message was not altered in any way during transmission. To learn more about digital IDs, visit the VeriSign Web site.*

Services that use digital IDs

  USPS EPM Extension for Microsoft Office allows users to sign Word documents digitally and then seal them with the USPS Electronic Postmark (EPM). After installing the EPM Extension, just click the blue eagle icon in your Microsoft Word toolbar, apply a USPS EPM to your document (contract, letter, or agreement), and electronically sign. This gives your document tamper protection against fraud, and it gives the recipient the ability to verify document authenticity online. Transaction records about postmarked Word documents are stored in the USPS EPM repository for seven years, providing third-party evidence to support non-repudiation of content. To learn more and download the software, visit the USPS EPM Web site.*

Figure 12-3 Digital ID Screen

1. The best known is VeriSign. Click on that link and follow the instructions provided. As of the writing of this book, there was a free 60-day trial for a VeriSign key and it was $14.95 per year.

2. After signing up, you will receive an e-mail from VeriSign. Click the Continue button in that e-mail (or as instructed) to move on to the next step of setting up a Digital ID.

3. This process now moves back to VeriSign's web site. Click on the Install button you see there to continue. The web page will inform you when it has finished installing the certificate. Now it is time to tell Outlook to utilize it.

4. Go back to the Tools–Options–Security tab within Outlook. Check the top two boxes (Encrypt contents and attachments ..., Add digital signatures ...) and click Apply.

5. With the certificate installed, a new e-mail will have these two icons 🔒🔒 in one of the toolbars. Clicking on these icons toggles message encryption and the addition of the digital signature.

You may be asking yourself "Do I need to get a Digital ID for my e-mails?" If your normal use of Outlook is just sending personal e-mail and/or joke e-mail to friends and relatives, the best decision is NO. Do you use e-mail for confidential business communication? Does it need to be verifiable and to guarantee that the received version is identical to the one sent? If so, you should get a Digital ID. And yes, it is worth the extra money for these uses.

Backing up and Restoring Data

This section goes through downloading, installing, and using the Personal Folders Backup utility. It shows you how to back up selected mailbox files at whatever interval you choose.

1. In your web browser, go to http://office.microsoft.com/home/.

2. Click on the Downloads link on the left side of the page.

3. Click on Downloads For Office 2003.

4. In the Outlook 2003 section, click on Add-ins.

5. Click on PST Backup.

6. Click Download.

7. Click Open.

8. Once in the installer, click Next to begin.

9. Read the license agreement and click that you accept it.

10. Click Next twice.

11. Click Finish when the installation is complete.

Once PST Backup has finished installing, you will need to close Outlook if you had it running during the download.

1. Open Outlook.
2. Click File and then Backup.
3. Click Options.
4. Check which files are to be backed up and how often and click OK.
5. Click Save Backup.

Note that if you choose to back up the main delivery location, you will be notified that the backup will be performed the next time you exit Outlook. The backup routine runs rather quickly. Now that the file has been backed up, you can restore it (if necessary) by importing it from the location where you stored the backup. Follow these steps:

1. Click File and then Import and Export.
2. Import from another program or file, click Next.
3. Personal folders file (.pst), click Next.
4. Either type in the location or browse to it. The default location should be something like `C:\Documents and Settings\SLink\ Local Settings\Application Data\Microsoft\Outlook\` and the file will be named something similar to `OutlookHotmail (1)-00000007 backup.pst`.

Now that you have mastered the procedure to back up and restore your Outlook data, you need to know one of the negatives of this type of backup procedure. If your hard drive crashes and the data on it is irretrievable, your Outlook backup is also gone.

The best recommendation is to point these backups to another drive in your system. An even better option is to make the destination location removable media such as zip disk, CDRW, or DVD-RW. Using this method the media can be stored away from the computer so that even a fire would not compromise your backups.

Password Protecting Your Mailbox

Does your mailbox contain sensitive e-mail? It may be stuff that your kids should not be able to view. Outlook can be configured to require a password to open the mailbox file.

Click Tools–Options–Mail Setup tab, and then Data Files. The following screen displays.

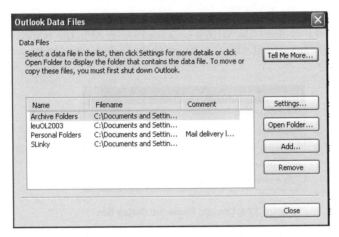

Figure 12-4 Outlook Data files Screen

Select the desired file and click on Settings to display the next screen.

Notice the format line in the Personal folders screen. Outlook 2003 has a new format available for the mailbox file. Although this new format was introduced with the 2003 version it is also able to create and read in the old format. The new format is called Office Outlook Personal Folders File. The file shown below is in the old format.

Figure 12-5 Personal Folders File

Clicking on the Change Password button lets you assign or change the password on the mailbox file. With a password assigned to the mailbox, the user will be presented with the screen shown below every time Outlook starts.

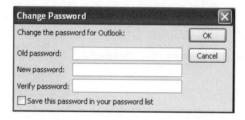

Figure 12-6 Change Password Dialog Box

13. Troubleshooting Outlook

Are there problems when running Outlook? Maybe you can't delete a calendar appointment or there are problems with the folder structure. This section provides the resources for troubleshooting and fixing most Outlook problems.

Detect and Repair

The first resource for troubleshooting resides on the Outlook Help menu. It is called Detect and Repair. This will check your Outlook installation for missing or corrupted files and fix them. It should fix most problems you might encounter. If you have run Detect and Repair and the problems are not fixed, refer to the startup switch references below.

Command Line Switches

First, let's go over the basics. The command line that starts Microsoft Outlook is Outlook.exe. Placing a forward slash (/) followed by the switch name and any parameters for the switch executes the desired functionality of that switch.

1. Search for the Outlook executable file, Outlook.exe, and make a note of its path. The default path is:

    `C:\Program Files\Microsoft Office\Office11\Outlook.exe`

2. Click Start, and then click Run.

3. In the Open box, type the complete path written down from step 1, including the file name. Press the spacebar once, and then type a forward slash (/) followed by the switch.

4. To run the command, click OK.

Note that some of the switches have the notation *For Advanced Users* beside them. The reason they are tagged as advanced is that they generally relate to Exchange Server or Collaboration Data Objects (CDO), and most users won't want to use them without specific instructions to do so.

For example, if you want to use the FIRSTRUN switch, the command you type in the Open box should look like this:

```
"C:\Program Files\Microsoft Office\Office11\Outlook.exe"
/Cleanreminders
```

Paths that include spaces between words must be enclosed in quotation marks (") and are case sensitive. This is the reason for the quotes around the command line shown above. Switches do not go in quotes.

The switches and their functions are listed below.

➢ /a

Creates an item with the specified file as an attachment.

Example:

"C:\Program Files\Microsoft Office/Office11/Outlook.exe" /a "C:\YourFile.doc"

If no item type is specified, IPM.Note (see /c below for item type explanation) is used. IPM.Note cannot be used with message classes that aren't based on Outlook.

➢ /altvba otmfilename – *For Advanced Users*

Opens the VBA program specified in otmfilename, rather than VbaProject.otm.

➢ /autorun macroname – *For Advanced Users*

Opens Outlook and immediately runs the macro specified in macroname.

➢ /c messageclass

Creates a new item of the specified message class (Outlook forms or any other valid MAPI form).

Examples:

/c ipm.activity creates a new Journal entry
/c ipm.appointment creates a new calendar entry
/c ipm.contact creates a new contact
/c ipm.note creates a new e-mail message
/c ipm.stickynote creates a new note
/c ipm.task creates a new task

➢ /checkclient

Prompts for the default manager of e-mail, news, and contacts. This is useful if you need to change the program automatically opened for e-mail.

➢ /cleanclientrules

Deletes rules that have been set up within Outlook. Use this with caution since it will remove all of your rules. If you have some that you want to keep, write them down before running this switch.

➢ /cleandmrecords *For Advanced Users*

Deletes the logging records saved when a manager or a delegate declines a meeting.

➢ /cleanfinders *For Advanced Users*

Removes Search Folders from the Microsoft Exchange server store.

➢ /cleanfreebusy

Clears and regenerates free/busy information. This switch can only be used when you are able to connect to your Microsoft Exchange server.

➢ /cleanprofile

Removes invalid profile keys and recreates default registry keys where applicable.

➢ /cleanpst

Launches Outlook with a clean Personal Folders file (.pst), which is the data file that stores your messages and other items on your computer. You can assign a .pst file to be the default delivery location for e-mail messages. You can also use a .pst to organize and back up items for safekeeping.

➢ /cleanreminders

Clears and regenerates reminders.

➢ /cleanrules

Starts Outlook and deletes client- and server-based rules.

➢ /cleanschedplus

Deletes all Schedule+ data (free/busy, permissions, and .cal file) from the server and enables the free/busy information from the Outlook Calendar to be used and viewed by all Schedule+ 1.0 users.

➢ /cleanserverrules *For Advanced Users*

Starts Outlook and deletes server-based rules.

➢ /cleansniff

Deletes duplicate reminder messages.

➢ /cleansubscriptions

Deletes the subscription messages and properties for subscription features.

➢ /cleanviews

Restores default views. All custom views you created are lost.

➢ /designer

Starts Outlook without figuring out if Outlook should be the default client in the first run.

➢ /embedding *For Advanced Users*

Opens the specified message file (.msg) as an OLE embedding. Also used without command line parameters for standard OLE co-create.

➢ /explorer

Opens the new window in Explorer mode (link bar on).

➢ /f msgfilenam

Opens the specified message file (.msg) or Microsoft Office saved search (.oss).

➢ /firstrun

Starts Outlook as if it were running for the first time.

➢ /folder

Opens a new window in Folder mode (Navigation Pane off).

➢ /hol holfilename *For Advanced Users*

Opens the specified .hol file.

➢ /ical icsfilename *For Advanced Users*

Opens the specified .ics file.

➢ /importprf prffilename

Launches Outlook and opens/imports the defined MAPI profile (*.prf). If Outlook is already open, queues the profile to be imported on the next clean launch.

➢ /l olkfilename *For Advanced Users*

Opens the specified .olk file.

➢ /launchtraininghelp assetid

Opens a Help window with the Help topic specified in *assetid*.

➢ /m e-mailname

Provides a way for the user to add an e-mail name to the item; only works in conjunction with the /c command-line parameter.

Example:

Outlook.exe /c ipm.note /m *e-mailname*

> `/nocustomize`

Starts Outlook without loading outcmd.dat (customized toolbars) and *.fav file.

> `/noextensions`

Starts Outlook with extensions turned off, but listed in the Add-In Manager.

> `/nopollmail`

Starts Outlook without checking mail at startup.

> `/nopreview`

Starts Outlook with the Reading Pane off and removes the option from the View menu.

> `/p msgfilename`

Prints the specified message (.msg). Does not work with HTML.

> `/profile profilename`

Loads the specified profile. If your profile name contains a space, enclose the profile name in quotation marks (").

> `/profiles`

Opens the Choose Profile dialog box regardless of the Options setting on the Tools menu.

> `/recycle`

Starts Outlook using an existing Outlook window, if one exists. Used in combination with the /explorer or /folder switch.

> `/resetfoldernames`

Resets default folder names (such as Inbox or Sent Items) to default names in the current Office user interface language.

For example, if you first connect to your mailbox Outlook using a Russian user interface, the Russian default folder names cannot be renamed. To change the default folder names to another language such as Japanese or English, you can use this switch to reset the default folder names after changing the user interface language or installing a different language version of Outlook.

> `/resetfolders`

Restores missing folders for the default delivery location.

> `/resetnavpane`

Clears and regenerates the Navigation Pane for the current profile.

➤ `/rpcdiag` For Advanced Users

Opens Outlook and displays the remote procedure call (RPC) connection status dialog.

➤ `/s filename`

Loads the specified shortcuts file (.fav).

➤ `/safe`

Starts Outlook without extensions, Reading Pane, or toolbar customization.

➤ `/safe:1`

Starts Outlook with the Reading Pane off.

➤ `/safe:2`

Starts Outlook without checking mail at startup.

➤ `/safe:3`

Starts Outlook with extensions turned off, but listed in the Add-In Manager.

➤ `/safe:4`

Starts Outlook without loading Outcmd.dat (customized toolbars) and *.fav file.

➤ `/select foldername`

Starts Outlook and opens the specified folder in a new window. For example, to open Outlook and display the default calendar use: `"c:\Program Files\Microsoft Office\Office11\Outlook.exe" /select outlook:calendar`

➤ `/sniff`

Starts Outlook and forces a detection of new meeting requests in the Inbox, and then adds them to the calendar.

➤ `/t oftfilename`

Opens the specified .oft file. OFT is the Outlook template. It could be pre-filled e-mail, a pre-set calendar item, or pretty much anything imaginable.

➤ `/v vcffilename`

Opens the specified .vcf file. VCF is a VCard file. It may be a contact item that has been saved as a vCalendar.

➢ `/vcal vcsfilename`

Opens the specified .vcs file. VCS is a vCalendar file. It may be a calendar item that has been saved as a vCalendar.

➢ `/x xnkfilename`

Opens the specified .xnk file. XNK is an Outlook Shortcut file.

Although all of the command line settings are listed for reference purposes, it is not expected that the average user will have a use for all of them. The most useful startup switches are:

➢ CleanFreeBusy

➢ CleanProfile

➢ CleanReminders

➢ CleanRules

➢ CleanViews

➢ FirstRun

➢ ResetFolders

➢ ResetNavPane

➢ Safe: (with 1,2,3, or 4 also)

Notice the overall purpose of these is CLEAN or RESET. If your Outlook starts to behave erratically, these switches could be of great use.

Inbox Repair Tool

A tool that you can us to recover your mailbox is called ScanPST. It is generally located at

`C:\Program Files\Common Files\System\Msmapi\1033`

This location could vary if Outlook is installed in a custom location or the default language on the system is not US English.

The First rule to keep in mind when running recovery tools on any file is to make a copy of the file before attempting to repair it. The possibility exists that instead of repairing whatever problems exist it could make them worse. If the repair does not seem to have worked, the original, untouched file still remains.

You need to know the location of the mailbox file before you run ScanPST. You can discover this by clicking Start, Search and looking for *.PST.

Troubleshooting and Managing Outlook Views

This section will be helpful if your information does not appear as you expect it to. The reason for this could be missing buttons, a filter set incorrectly, incorrect views, and so on. Some of the terms I use may require explanation.

Missing Buttons

Problem	Solution
I can't rename a view because the Rename button is disabled.	➤ If the current view is a standard view, you cannot rename it. Instead, copy the standard view, give it a new name, and then change the settings if you haven't already customized the view the way you want.
My Address Bar is missing.	➤ To go to a Web site, you can pull up your browser and type the address in. If you would rather skip these few extra clicks, you can use the Address Bar to go to a Web site. Click the View menu, point to Toolbars, click Web. Now that the address bar is displayed in Outlook, you can type the (web or local) address there.
The button I want is not in the Navigation Pane.	➤ To add or remove buttons in the Navigation Pane, click Configure Buttons ▪ (generally located in the bottom right corner of the Navigation Pane). Click Add or Remove Buttons, and then click the button you want.

Tip: To rearrange the buttons displayed in the Navigation Pane, click Configure Buttons, and then click Navigation Pane Options. Find the Display buttons in this order list; click the button you want to change, and then click Move Up or Move Down.

Disappearing Items

Problem	Solution
Items disappear when switching to another view.	➤ Some items in a folder may be temporarily hidden if the view you are using includes a filter. To see all of the items, remove the filter.

Removing a Filter

1. On the View menu, point to Arrange By, and then click Custom.
2. Click Filter.
3. Click Clear All.

> Tip: You can quickly tell if a view filter has been applied to a folder by checking to see if the status bar displays the words Filter Applied in the lower-left corner of the screen. Multiple Filters Applied indicates that both a synchronization filter and a view filter have been applied. A synchronization filter allows you to choose which items are downloaded or kept in your Offline Folder Files

Can't Edit Items

Problem	Solution
I can't edit my items.	➢ Some fields cannot be edited directly in a card view type. For example, you cannot edit the contact name in the card heading or the contents of the Notes field. To edit this information, you must open the contact.
	➢ You may have switched to a view in which editing is off. In a card or table view type, you can switch editing on or off. See Toggling Editing On and Off below.
	➢ You may have changed to a multi-line layout. In-cell editing cannot be done in multi-line layout, and when you change from single-line layout to multi-line layout, in-cell editing is automatically turned off. If you switch to single-line layout, in-cell editing will be automatically turned back on.

Toggling Editing On and Off

1. On the View menu, point to Arrange By, Current View, and then click Customize Current View.
2. Click Other Settings.
3. Select or clear the Allow in-cell editing check box.

Text Displays Incorrectly

Using automatic formatting, only the first line of my message displays correctly.	➤ In multi-line layout, automatic formatting rules apply only to the first line of text. Switch to single-line layout if you want all the lines of your message to be automatically formatted.

Missing Shortcuts

Problem	Solution
I have created a new group and my new shortcut doesn't show there.	➤ By default, new shortcuts that you create will always be added to the shortcut group. Click the shortcut you added, and then drag it to the new group you created.

Problems with Views

Problem	Solution
The view I created is not shown.	➤ When you create a custom view, the view is added to the Current View submenu. To switch to the new view, on the View menu, point to Arrange By, Current View, and then click the view you want.
	➤ A view can only be used for the same type of folder it was created for. For example, if you create a view for Inbox, you can't use it for Tasks. To use the same view settings, you must create another view in Tasks.
	➤ You can set a custom view to be available in the current folder or in all folders of the same type; for example, all Contacts folders. The view you want to use may not be available in the folder you are in. Switch to the folder you created the view in, copy the view, and then change where it can be used.

I added columns to a
Table view but I can't
see all of them.

> Microsoft Outlook automatically resizes all
column headings in the Table view to fit in
the Outlook window. That way you don't have
to scroll to see the columns. In multi-line
layout, Outlook displays only a few fields or
columns; however you can see more by
changing the number of lines that display.
You can also see more columns by switching
to single-line layout.

The current view pane
no longer shows folder
views.

> You have selected the Only show views
created for this folder check box in the
Custom View Organizer dialog box.
To display the views on the View menu, point
to Arrange By, Current View, and then click
Define Views. Clear the Only show views
created for this folder check box.

Can't Copy Information Because Field Is Not Displayed

I want to copy
information from a field
that isn't displayed.

> You need to display the field in the current
view, verify that in-cell editing is turned on,
and then copy its contents. See below for
details.

Copying Information from a Field That Is Not Displayed

1. On the View menu, point to Arrange By, Current View, and then
   click a table view type.

2. Add the columns whose contents you want to copy to the view.

> Tip: In a table, a field is a column that contains information. In a card, a field is a
> box with a label that contains information.

3. On the View menu, point to Arrange By, and then click Custom.

4. Click Fields.

5. Do one of the following:

   a) Add a field or column

   b) In the Available fields box, click the field you want to add.

   c) If the field you want is not in the Available fields box, click a different field set in the Select available fields from box, and then click a field.

6. Click Add.

Removing a Field or Column from View

1. In the Show these fields in this order box, click the field you want to remove.

2. Click Remove.

> Tip: To quickly remove a column, drag the column heading away from the row until an X appears through the column heading, ▭▭ Start ✖▭▭ and then release the mouse button.

Enabling In-cell Editing and Text Copying

1. On the View menu, point to Arrange By, and then click Custom.

2. Click Other Settings.

3. Select the Allow in-cell editing check box, and then click OK.

4. Select the text you want to copy.

5. On the Edit menu, click Copy.

6. Switch to the other program or to the item where you want to copy the information.

7. On the Edit menu, click Paste.

Multi-line Layout Doesn't Make Sense

Problem	Solution
The information in my multi-line layout doesn't make sense.	➤ Multi-line layout normally displays four fields (From, Subject, Date, and Icon). If you have changed the order of the fields (columns) or added a text field to the column order before the From or Subject fields, your message information may display incorrectly in multi-line layout.

Switch to single-line layout and review and rearrange your column headings. The fields should be ordered so that From and Subject are the first two text fields, and the Date field (Received or Sent) is the first date field. You can specify that additional fields appear on lines following these default fields.

This page intentionally left blank.

14. Talking to Outlook

I am sure you have seen movies where people talk to a computer and it responds. That is actually possible in the recent Outlook versions.

Once the voice capacity is installed, the following toolbar will be displayed in the foreground of speech-capable applications (such as Word, Excel, Outlook, and many others).

Figure 14-1 Voice Command Toolbar

Of course, you need a microphone. A standard headset microphone (with noise cancellation) works great for this purpose. As a matter of fact, I am speaking to the computer at this moment. It has only missed one word so far, when it put "had" instead of "at" in the previous sentence.

Clicking on the Microphone button activates the microphone to send dictation or commands. It is quite easy to switch from one mode to the other; just click on the corresponding button. Voice commands such as Cut, Paste, Copy, and Undo can be used in combination with highlighting with the mouse to easily edit an e-mail.

The Speak button will actually read a passage that is highlighted. If that passage was dictated to the computer, it is played in the actual voice that recorded it. If it reads typed text, the voice is a computerized voice of your choosing.

Giving Your Computer a Voice

Click Start, Control Panel, Speech, and the Text to Speech tab to open the following screen.

Figure 14-2 Selecting Speech Properties

This is where you select a default voice. The three default choices are shown in the drop down box. Once you choose a voice, the computer tells you in that voice which "person" you have chosen. You can also set the voice speed here.

Training the Speech Module

You train the computer to recognize your speech patterns and words by reading books to it. The minimum training time that you should expect is thirty minutes.

You will be reading literature such as Aesop's Fables and The Wonderful Wizard of Oz so that the computer can learn to recognize your voice. There are eight default stories to choose from. Better and more accurate speech recognition comes from reading as many of these stories as time will allow.

You can read them all at once if you can stand it, or just one or two at a time. Click on the Tools button on the speech bar shown above to perform additional training (see Figure 14-1).

Although training provides a more accurate start, the system also learns an individual's speech patterns with use. You will notice that the accuracy improves as you used it more and more.

Like everything else that is computer related, the speech module can be customized. Click on the Tools button (on the speech bar) and then Options. The screen shown below will appear.

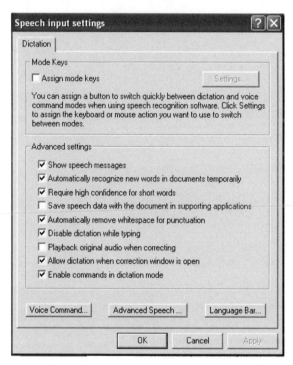

Figure 14-3 Changing Speech Input Settings

Now it will become a habit to talk to your computer even if you don't have the headset on.

This page intentionally left blank.

15. Instant Messaging

Do you have friends who are active with Windows Instant Messenger? Wish you could join them?

Setting up an account is easy and free. As a matter of fact, if you already have a Hotmail account, half of the job is done. In this section we will cover setting up a Hotmail account and linking that to Instant Messenger.

Take a look at the Start bar. There is probably an icon that looks like a little green man.

Double click on it; a Windows Messenger screen appears. If your system has never been set up for WM, the next thing to do is click on the link to sign in. Click Next on the .Net Passport Wizard opening screen.

The next screen asks if you have an e-mail address. For security purposes many people don't want to associate their "regular" e-mail address with an Instant Messaging account, so we will choose to create a new Hotmail account. Select No and click Next twice.

Now the default web browser opens to the Hotmail registration screen (see below) and allows you to create a new e-mail address.

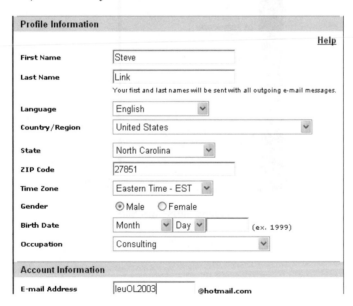

Figure 15-1 Registering a New Hotmail Account

Notice that the secret question and other security information are omitted from the screen. It would be a quite negligent to publish everything about your e-mail addresses for the world to see!

Fill in all the information and click on the I Agree button. The Windows Messaging wizard then comes back into play. Click Next to associate the Passport information with the Windows user account. At last, everything is set up and you are in the world of Instant Messaging!

Make note of my e-mail address and Messenger ID, `leuOL2003@Hotmail.com`. If you have any questions, comments, or have need of further explanation of topics covered here, feel free to e-mail or IM me at this address. The Windows Messenger screen is shown below.

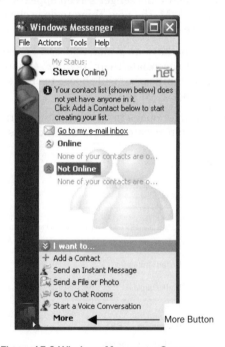

Figure 15-2 Windows Messenger Screen

Click on Add a Contact to add all of your friends and start chatting (and More).

Saving a Conversation

If there has been a lengthy conversation and you need to save it for future reference, you can click File and then Save As in the conversation window. Outlook saves the conversation in a plain text file readable by Windows Notepad, Word, or any other text editor.

The More Button

You now have the ability to send a file or photo, have a voice conversation, and more. Clicking on the More option allows you to share an electronic whiteboard with other users. An example is shown below.

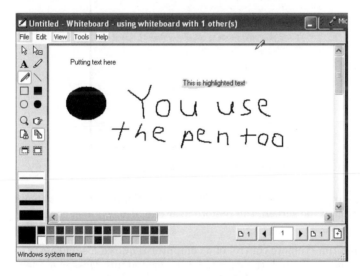

Figure 15-3 Whiteboard Screen

Choose which online user to start a whiteboard conversation with and click OK to begin.

Whatever is entered on one whiteboard is shown on the other. This appears as a standard Paint screen. You can type, draw, highlight, etc. The option for saving the screen is also available.

Application sharing is also available under More. Choose a user and click OK. Once the user accepts the invitation, choose which application to share (shown on the following page).

Figure 15-4 Sharing an Application

Choose the application to share and click on the Share button. As shown at the bottom of the screen, the remote user can also be given control of the host system.

Once upon a time remote control of a computer required a separate program to be purchased. It seems to be integrated into Messenger very nicely, if used through a fast Internet connection.

16. Using Newsgroups

Internet Newsgroups are A valuable source for information. The newsgroup viewer used is actually Outlook Express. Your Internet Service Provider (ISP) should have provided the addresses for their newsgroup servers upon signup. In this section, we will go through the procedure of setting up the newsgroup information and using one of the Microsoft Outlook newsgroups.

News is not a default button on the standard toolbar (which generally has Print, Send/Receive, etc.). In a previous section, we covered customizing toolbars and menus (see page 5-2). This is a good time to practice the procedures learned there to add the News button to the standard toolbar. The procedure will be explained here, but refer to the previous customization section for exact screenshots.

1. Click on the Tools menu, Customize, and the Commands tab. Click on Go (on the left side) and scroll in the list until News is displayed.

2. Click on News and drag it to the toolbar where you want to add it. Now that the News button has been added, click on it any time to view the subscribed newsgroups.

3. Next, click on News, connect to the Microsoft news server, and subscribe to their Outlook newsgroup.

4. With Outlook Newsreader opened, click on Tools and Accounts. The following screen should display. Click on the Add button in the upper right corner.

Figure 16-1 Adding a News Account

5. Click on News to pull up the Internet Connection Wizard. Enter the user information as requested. Since newsgroups are "farmed" for e-mail addresses, it is suggested that you enter a pseudonym for the name field and enter a modified e-mail address.

    For instance, to ward off unwanted spam, I might enter the e-mail address spkill_leuOL2003@hotmail.com. A real person who wants to send e-mail to this address will be able to remove the added seven characters, but the automated address programs will not be able to accomplish that feat. Also, do not use standard words such as NOSPAM (or similar) because the e-mail farming programs can be easily set to clean that up.

6. The news server being used is news.microsoft.com. That news server does not require log on, so leave the check box empty. When prompted, click Finish to add the news server.

7. Click on Tools and Newsgroups. A screen similar to the one shown below appears.

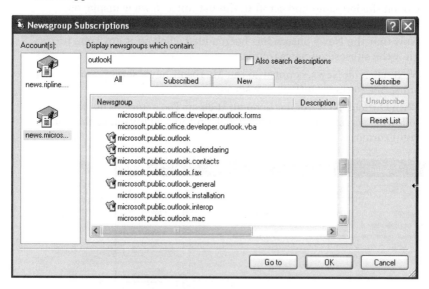

Figure 16-2 Adding a News Server

The highlighted account is news.microsoft.com, and the Newsgroup listing displays all newsgroups that contain the word "outlook". Notice the folder icon beside of some of the newsgroups. This indicates the newsgroups to which you have subscribed; the list of new messages is shown in bold in the Newsreader program.

Posting to a Newsgroup

Posting a message in a newsgroup is basically the same procedure as sending an e-mail. Click on the New Post button (generally in the upper left corner) to create a new posting to the newsgroup. The screen pictured below will display.

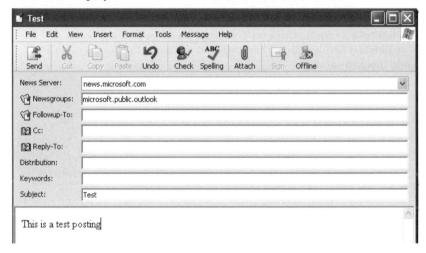

Figure 16-3 Posting a Newsgroup Message

The news server and newsgroup are already filled in, but you can change them if necessary. This message can also be sent to other e-mail addresses by placing them in the CC field. Type your subject and message. Click Send to post it. A message may display as a reminder that your message may not appear immediately in the newsgroups. See the following screen for a sample screen shot and posting.

0	↓	⁰ͨ	Subject	From	Sent	Size
			Re: Strips attachments when forwarding...	Phoenix	1/24/2004 4:50...	1KB
			Re: Syc Outlook	Thomas Wetzel	1/25/2004 4:24...	1KB
			Re: Sync "Sent Items" on two computers	Thomas Wetzel	1/25/2004 4:22...	1KB
			synchronizing outlook with my mob	Antonio	1/25/2004 7:16...	1KB
		⊞	syncing multiple handhelds to the same ...	anonymous@discussion...	12/20/2003 10:...	1KB
			Tasks and Reminders	William	1/24/2004 9:54...	1KB
			Test	Steve Link	1/25/2004 6:59...	1KB
		⊞	Test message	JamesD	1/25/2004 3:36...	1KB
			The item has been moved or deleted - M...	rameshkuamrp	12/20/2003 4:0...	2KB
		⊞	The Private box on the contact card in ...	Gregory V	12/20/2003 12:...	1KB
			Re: Transfer Outlook data to a new com...	Milly Staples [MVP - Out...	1/24/2004 6:25...	1KB
		⊞	transfering Outlook contacts from one c...	Pete	1/16/2004 1:49...	1KB

Figure 16-4 Screen Shot Showing Posted Message

The highlighted posting appeared less than 15 minutes after posting it. Notice that I didn't change the name before sending the message so it is properly displayed.

Although the newsgroups provide a wide area for abuse by spammers and others, they also provide a great amount of help from highly qualified individuals (Outlook MVPs, for example).

A useful security measure (just like Junk Senders list) is the ability to block newsgroup senders. Click on Tools and Message Rules. Choose News or Blocked Senders list. These work in the same fashion as e-mail rules and blocked senders.

17. Are You Certifiable?

After using Outlook and the Office Suite you may decide that it is time to get a certificate that confirms what you know. That is where Certification programs come into the picture.

There are three levels of certification available – Specialist, Expert, and Master. These are available for the Office 2000, 2002, and 2003 versions, although the 2003 certification was not ready as of the writing of this book. The specifications of the levels are explained below.

Outlook Specialist

It is required that you know how to:

- Create and view messages
- Manage messages
- Properly utilize scheduling
- Create and manage contacts, tasks, and notes

Specialist certification is available for Word, Excel, PowerPoint, Access, and Outlook. One exam covers each program and results in an individual certificate.

Expert

The Expert certification level includes only Word and Excel. The exams for this level are more advanced than those in the Specialist level. The requirements are shown below.

Word

It is required that you know how to:

- Customize paragraphs
- Format documents
- Customize tables
- Create and modify graphics
- Customize Word
- Perform workgroup collaboration
- Use mail merge.

Excel

It is required that you know how to:

> Import and export
> Managing workbooks
> Formatting numbers
> Work with ranges
> Customize Excel
> Audit worksheets
> Summarize data
> Analyze data
> Perform workgroup collaboration.

Master

This is the highest level of certification you can achieve. The previous levels include one test and one certification achieved. In order to acquire Master certification, exams are required in Word, Excel, and PowerPoint. Additionally, you need to take an exam in either Access or Outlook.

There are two versions of the Word, Excel, and PowerPoint exams. These are the Specialist level and the Expert/Master level exams. The Specialist exams on Access and Outlook also apply for completion of the Master requirements.

The allotted time for each exam is 45 minutes and consists of 21-24 questions involving 49-56 tasks. See the web page below for more information on local testing locations.

    http://www.microsoft.com/learning/mcp/officespecialist/

One Raleigh, NC testing center charges $65 per test. This price may vary.

Since the subject of this book is Outlook, there are twelve examples of Outlook 2002 exam questions below, three from each of the four different areas mentioned above.

E-mail

1. When searching for a word in an e-mail, you can search through: (select all that apply)
   a. A specific folder
   b. All mail folders
   c. Sent mail
   d. Received mail
   e. Inbox

2. An automatic send/receive can be scheduled when Outlook is: (only one answer is correct)
   a. Online
   b. Offline
   c. Both
   d. Neither

3. What is the limit to the number of subfolders that can be assigned? (only one answer is correct)
   a. 3
   b. 5
   c. 7
   d. No limit

Calendar

1. Circle the names of correct calendar views (circle all that apply)
   a. Day
   b. Week
   c. Month
   d. Year
   e. Workweek

2. True or false: The only method of calendar sharing is through Exchange Server.

3. Which of these reminder settings are correct?
   a. 5 minutes
   b. 12 minutes
   c. 6 hours
   d. 1 week

Contacts

1. How many different phone numbers are available for a single contact?
    a. 6
    b. 10
    c. 15
    d. 19
    e. Any number
2. True or false: You can add a contact's picture to their record.
3. What is the shortest procedure for mapping the address of a contact?
    a. Go to www.mappoint.com and enter the address
    b. Use a road map and highlighter
    c. Click the "Display map of address" button
    d. Click the "Map-It" button

Tasks

1. Which of these views show the percent completion of a task? (circle all that apply)
    a. Simple List
    b. Detailed list
    c. Active tasks
    d. Overdue tasks
    e. Assignment
2. Can an e-mail easily be turned into a task?
3. Will a task that is set for monthly recurrence automatically end after twelve occurrences?

Answers

E-mail
1 – a,b,c,d,e
2 – c
3 – d

Calendar
1 – a,b,c,e
2 – False
3 – a,c,d

Contacts
1 – e
2 – True
3 – c

Tasks
1 – b,c
2 – Yes
3 – No

Appendix A

Keyboard Shortcuts

If you would prefer to use the keyboard for all of your commands, you can do it. In this section, you'll become acquainted with ways to use most of the functions within Outlook from the keyboard.

This appendix is divided into various sections, with the shortcuts that apply listed in each section. Many of these work also in other programs within the Office 2003 suite.

Shortcuts for the Help Pane

Shortcut	Action
TAB	Move forward one item within the Help Pane (Next)
SHIFT TAB	Back up one item within the Help Pane (Previous)
ENTER	Perform the action associated with the highlighted item
DOWN ARROW	Scroll down through the Help Pane
UP ARROW	Scroll up through the Help Pane
ALT LEFT ARROW	Open the previous Help Pane
ALT RIGHT ARROW	Open the next Help Pane
CTRL SPACE	Open the Help Pane options menu
CTRL F1	Open or close the Help Task Pane

Shortcuts for the Help Window

Shortcut	Action
TAB	Select the next hyperlink
SHIFT TAB	Select the previous hyperlink
ENTER	Perform the action associated with the highlighted item

Shortcut	Action
ALT RIGHT ARROW	Open the next help topic
ALT LEFT ARROW	Open the previous help topic
CTRL P	Print the selected help topic
ALT U	Alternate between "tiled" and "untiled" mode within the help window

Shortcuts for General Menu and Toolbar

Shortcut	Action
F10	Toggle selection/deselection of the menu bar
TAB	Go to the next item on the toolbar
SHIFT TAB	Go to the previous item on the toolbar
CTRL TAB	Select the next toolbar
CTRL SHIFT TAB	Select the previous toolbar
ENTER	Open the highlighted menu or perform the selected action
SHIFT F10	Display a shortcut menu for the highlighted item
ALT SPACE	Selected window shortcut menu
HOME	Go to the first item in a menu
END	Go to the last item in a menu
ESC	Close the currently open menu
CTRL DOWN ARROW	Display all commands within the menu
CTRL ESC	Bring up the Start menu

Shortcuts for Basic Outlook Navigation

Shortcut	Action
CTRL 1	Go to Mail Pane
CTRL 2	Go to Calendar Pane
CTRL 3	Go to Contacts Pane

Shortcut	Action
CTRL 4	Go to Tasks Pane
CTRL 5	Go to Notes Pane
CTRL 6	Go to Navigation Pane Folder List
CTRL 7	Go to Navigation Pane Shortcuts List
F6	Switch to another pane
TAB	Move between the main Outlook window, Navigation Pane, and Reading Pane
CTRL Y	Select Outlook folder to be opened

Shortcuts for Item Creation and Manipulation

Shortcut	Action
CTRL SHIFT A	New Appointment
CTRL SHIFT C	New Contact
CTRL SHIFT E	New folder
CTRL SHIFT H	New Document
CTRL SHIFT J	New Journal entry
CTRL SHIFT K	New Task
CTRL SHIFT L	New Distribution List
CTRL SHIFT M	New Message
CTRL SHIFT N	New Note
CTRL SHIFT Q	New Meeting Request
CTRL SHIFT S	Post item in the selected folder
CTRL SHIFT U	New Task Request
CTRL SHIFT X	New Fax
CTRL S	Save the item open on your screen
ALT S	Save and close the current item
F12	Save As
SHIFT F1	View screen tip

Shortcut	Action
CTRL D	Delete the current item
CTRL P	Print the current item
CTRL-Z	Undo the last function
CTRL SHIFT Y	Copy selected item(s)
CTRL SHIFT V	Move selected item(s)
F3	Open search toolbar
CTRL SHIFT F	Open Advanced Find
CTRL SHIFT P	Create Search Folder

Shortcuts for E-mail

Shortcut	Action
ALT K	Verify recipient names (Word as e-mail editor)
ALT S	Send message
CTRL F	Forward message
CTRL K	Verify recipient names (Outlook as e-mail editor)
CTRL Q	Mark as read
CTRL R	Reply
CTRL SHIFT B	Open address book
CTRL SHIFT G	Open Flag For Follow-up dialog
CTRL SHIFT I	Switch to Inbox
CTRL SHIFT O	Switch to Outbox
CTRL SHIFT R	Reply to all
CTRL SHIFT S	Post to selected folder
DOWN ARROW	Scroll down through messages
F7	Spell check message body
F9	Check for new mail (all accounts)
INSERT	Quick Flag selected message
UP ARROW	Scroll up through messages

Shortcuts for Appointment and Tasks

Shortcut	Action
ALT C	Accept meeting request
ALT D	Decline meeting request

Shortcuts for Contacts

Shortcut	Action
F11	Search for contact
CTRL SHIFT D	Dial phone number of contact

Shortcuts for Formatting Text

Shortcut	Action
ALT O	Open Format menu
SHIFT F3	Change case of selected text
CTRL B	Bold
CTRL SHIFT L	Change to bulleted item
CTRL I	Italicize
CTRL T	Increase indentation
CTRL SHIFT T	Decrease indentation
CTRL L	Left align
CTRL E	Center text
CTRL R	Right align
CTRL U	Underline
CTRL]	Increase font size
CTRL [	Decrease font size
CTRL X	Cut
CTRL C	Copy
CTRL V	Paste

Shortcut	Action
CTRL SHIFT Z	Clear all text formatting
CTRL LEFT CLICK	Edit a URL contained in the body of an item

Shortcuts for Working with Table Views

Shortcut	Action
ENTER	Open item
CTRL A	Select all
PAGE DOWN	Select the item at the bottom of the View Pane
PAGE UP	Select the item at the top of the View Pane
SHIFT DOWN ARROW	Extend a selected group by one
SHIFT UP ARROW	Shorten a selected group by one
CTRL DOWN ARROW	Next item without increasing the size of the list
CTRL UP ARROW	Previous item without shortening the list
CTRL SPACE	Toggle selection of the active item

Shortcuts for Working With Day/Week/Month Views

Shortcut	Action
ALT – (hyphen)	Switch to WEEKS view
ALT = (equals)	Switch to MONTHS view
ALT 0	View ten days starting with current
ALT 1 thru ALT 9	View multiple days
ALT DOWN ARROW	Date navigator, same day of next week
ALT DOWN ARROW	Day view, move item to same day and time a week later
ALT END	Date navigator, last day of week
ALT HOME	Date navigator, first day of week
ALT PAGE DOWN	Date navigator, last day of month
ALT PAGE UP	Date navigator, first day of month

Shortcut	Action
ALT UP ARROW	Date navigator, same day of last week
ALT UP ARROW	Day view, move item to same day and time a week earlier
DOWN ARROW	Next time section
END	Day view, end of the workday
END	Week or month view, last day of week
F6	Switch between Calendar, Taskpad, and Folder Lists
HOME	Day view, start of the workday
HOME	Week or month view, first day of week
PAGE DOWN (month view)	Same day five weeks later
PAGE DOWN (week view)	Same day of next week
PAGE UP (month view)	Same day five weeks earlier
PAGE UP (week view)	Same day or previous week
SHIFT DOWN ARROW	Increase selected time section
SHIFT TAB	Previous appointment
SHIFT UP ARROW	Decrease selected time section
TAB	Next appointment
UP ARROW	Previous time section

Shortcuts for Address Card Views

Shortcut	Action
UP ARROW	Previous address card
DOWN ARROW	Next address card
HOME	First address card
END	Last address card

Shortcut	Action
PAGE UP	Select the first address card on the page
PAGE DOWN	Select the last address card on the page
CTRL SPACE	Toggle selection of the currently highlighted address card
SHIFT HOME	Select from the current address card to the top
SHIFT END	Select from the current address card to the last
F2	Select the first field in the current address card
TAB	Move to the next field in the address card
SHIFT TAB	Move to the previous field in an address card

Index